HEAR MY SONG

Meditations on life
through favourite hymns

PAM RHODES

Illustrations by
Monica Capoferri

SPCK

First published in Great Britain in 2010

Society for Promoting Christian Knowledge
36 Causton Street
London SW1P 4ST

British Library Cataloguing-in-Publication Data
A catalogue record for this book is available from the British Library

ISBN 978–0–281–06193–8

1 3 5 7 9 10 8 6 4 2

Designed and typeset by Kenneth Burnley, Wirral, Cheshire
Printed in Great Britain by Ashford Colour Press

Produced on paper from sustainable forests

Contents

Introduction

I love hymns. It's not just because I've presented the BBC Television series *Songs of Praise* for more than twenty years and therefore probably know more hymns than most people have had hot dinners! The fact is I've always loved hymns. I loved singing them in Sunday school and in assembly, and I've loved singing them ever since.

It may be something to do with those unforgettable, stirring melodies – once sung, never forgotten. Who could fail to be moved by Handel's music for 'Thine Be the Glory', or Hubert Parry's 'Jerusalem'? How could you not be touched by the haunting tune for 'Abide with Me' or 'Be Thou My Vision'? Without a doubt, the marriage of words and music can sometimes be so sublime, it's impossible to think of one without the other.

But for me, it's the words that really count. I suppose it's because most hymn verses started off life as poems, often written at times of great inspiration, stress or emotion. It really doesn't matter if the writer was a psalmist putting pen to parchment three thousand years ago or a modern-day writer tapping away on a computer keyboard – the human condition has remained constant. We all recognize the same feelings – whether we're longing for comfort, protection, guidance, or just worn down by world-weariness; whether our daily lives have become a struggle, or we can't sleep at night because we are troubled by the problems of what seems to be a heartless world around us. Whatever we're going through, because we're human, we share the same emotions – and it's those emotions that have been expressed in graphic, lyrical, inspirational words by poets and hymn writers down the ages.

When I was growing up, I learned some of the great poems of the English language parrot-fashion in class, and even now most of those lines are still imprinted in my mind. The same goes for hymns. Mostly they are in rhyming couplets, which makes them easy to remember, and in addition we easily recall the music to which the words fit, so we just have to hear that melody again for the words to come flooding back. Sometimes the wording might sound a little strange or even archaic, but the sentiment shines through to strike chords in our own lives.

More than that, the words of so many hymns obviously started life as prayers. Often they are directed straight to God in praise or supplication, and you can imagine that the writers were filled with a sense of prayer as they wrote. On many occasions, writers have said that the words almost wrote themselves, as if by divine gift. Certainly, the conciseness of meaning and the depth of emotion expressed in short lines of verse can make some words simply unforgettable. You'll have your own favourites. But for me, the verses in this book have real power to comfort and inspire. Take, for instance, these enduring words, written by Henry Lyte, which speak so evocatively of how helpless we feel at times of great worry:

> **Abide with me; fast falls the eventide;**
> the darkness deepens: Lord, with me abide!
> when other helpers fail, and comforts flee,
> help of the helpless, O abide with me.

And what encouragement can be found when we are in a dark tunnel of pain and uncertainty from the words George Matheson wrote when he was in the swirls of depression:

> **O love that wilt not let me go,**
> I rest my weary soul in thee;
> I give thee back the life I owe,
> that in thine ocean depths its flow
> may richer, fuller be.

Because these favourites of mine are more than a century old, it's tempting to say, 'They don't write them like that any more' – but they do! Modern-day writers such as Stuart Townend, Dave Bilborough, John Bell and Graham Kendrick are wonderful wordsmiths whose songs are an outpouring of both their humanity and God's divinity, in just the same inspired way as the hymns of writers of years gone by.

Introduction

I like to think of this book as a spiritual first-aid kit. Take a look at the chapter headings, and on days when they seem to express exactly how you feel, dip into the pages and see what speaks to you. You'll find so much that you need here – challenge, comfort, hope, thanks and love. And maybe this book needs another chapter, the one you create yourself. What hymns have stayed with you over the years – and why? Do they bring back heart-warming memories? Do they remind you of emotional times in the past, or periods of particular challenge or fulfilment? Do they give you courage to face difficulty or disappointment? Do they make you think about your responsibilities to God's world and people? Do they give you a clearer picture of what God truly means to you? There are many questions voiced in the lines of these hymns, but so many more answers!

Cherish the hymns you love. Hold them dear. Keep them close to your heart. Draw strength from them – and don't be afraid to let others hear *your* song!

Pam Rhodes

One more step along the world I go

There's a little hymn I remember from my school days that often comes to mind nowadays. Do you remember this?

> **Glad that I live am I;**
> that the sky is blue;
> glad for the country lanes,
> and the fall of dew.
>
> After the sun the rain,
> after the rain, the sun,
> this is the way of life,
> till the work be done.

(Lizette Woodworth Reese, 1856–1935)

1

Mostly, it's just the first line that pops into my head at certain moments when I find myself feeling grateful just to be here, to have all I have and be what I am. I think of those times as 'Glad that I live am I!' moments – and I look back and count my blessings as I remember each and every one of them. I suppose that's because they are balanced against all the mundane, tiring, upsetting, frustrating or even downright difficult times that seem to fill the rest of each day. Is it just me, or does life generally seem more frantic, more trouble-some, more worrying with each succeeding year? For others, of course, it may be quite the opposite – that what worries them is having too much time on their hands as families move away and partnerships or work situations change, per-haps bringing loneliness and a lessening sense of worth. That's why I think those 'Glad that I live am I!' moments are important for all of us, especially as they often happen when you least expect them. For me, such moments come when I'm walking down the lane near home, for instance, and notice first the buds, then the blossom, then the berries in the hedgerow as the seasons change; or when I'm looking at the tiny, perfect fingers of a new grandchild; or getting my shoulders under hot water in a deep, sweet-smelling bath at the end of a long day; or in the company of good friends; or cooking a Sunday roast, then sitting round the table watch-ing the family eat with enthusiasm; or glancing up towards someone I care about, only to find they are already looking at me with a loving smile . . . There are so many moments, each mentioned in gratitude in my nightly prayers, then stored away in the warmest corner of my heart.

But for most of us, those heart-warming moments are fleeting in comparison with the ordinary stuff of life – work, bills, family, health, disputes, politics, the environment – all those worries that exhaust us by day, then keep us awake at night. It is those concerns that often make up a very long list of requests that we pour out to God in our prayers.

So in this chapter, I think we should recognize and value all the blessings of life – the obvious and significant alongside the most menial and everyday. For challenges that threaten to defeat us, we can pray for God's understanding and support – before we stand back to see the bigger picture, the rough and the smooth of our lives, and thank God for every glorious second.

Fill Thou My Life, O Lord My God

Praise in the common things of life,
　　its goings out and in;
praise in each duty and each deed,
　　however small and mean.

(Horatius Bonar, 1808–89)

This small verse, written by Horatius Bonar, who was a founder member of the Free Church of Scotland, sums up that sense of being thankful for even the most humble aspects of our lives, and wanting to show gratitude by doing our best with every task and situation, even those we don't enjoy much! That's a tall order because it would take nothing less than a saint to be humble and grateful for everything every day – but the sentiment is a good one because, whatever the challenges of your life, would you really prefer not to have had the gift of life at all? Life *is* a gift, and once given, it's ours to make what we want of it. That's the choice God allows us. Some days will be better than others. Some things may irritate or hurt us, but others bring us great pleasure. The secret is to value it all, treasure every precious moment because you have no idea how long – or short – your life is destined to be.

Lord of All Hopefulness, Lord of All Joy

Lord of all eagerness, Lord of all faith,
whose strong hands were skilled at the plane and the lathe,
be there at our labours, and give us, we pray,
your strength in our hearts, Lord, at the noon of the day.

(Jan Struther, 1901–53)

4

Jan Struther, also known by her Polish maiden name of Joyce Placzek, became well known at the start of the Second World War for writing the book *Mrs Miniver*, which was made into an inspirational and popular film. Then she turned her hand to writing hymn texts for the brand-new hymn book, *Songs of Praise*, which became a national favourite. She wrote words for well-known melodies – and her idea for the traditional tune 'Slane' was a hymn that tracked each day, from the moment we wake up hoping for God's bliss; then through the verse shown here, which asks for strength during our working hours; then God's love, hoped for in the welcome of our home-coming; and, lastly, for God's peace in our hearts at the end of the day.

I've chosen verse 2 because it's good to think that Christ can truly understand the challenges of our day. After all, he's been here too. He put in long hours as a carpenter. He needed skill, dedication and strength to get through every working day – and no doubt came home exhausted, just like us!

When morning gilds the skies,
my heart awaking cries,
    may Jesus Christ be praised:
alike at work and prayer
to Jesus I repair;
    may Jesus Christ be praised.

(German hymn, author unknown,
trans. Edward Caswall, 1814–78)

Because the human experience hasn't changed much down the years, whether the writer is a psalmist three thousand years ago or someone writing only yesterday, the wish to dedicate our time and talent to God is a recurring theme in hymn texts. Down the years, writers have wanted to express the simple joy of being co-workers with God in the business of life and the needs of the world around us. Edward Caswall was inspired to write his much-loved hymn when he discovered an earlier anonymous German poem that speaks of a wish to live and work for Christ as an expression of daily prayer.

Writing almost a century earlier, Charles Wesley shared his heartfelt prayer that everything he spoke, thought or worked to create should be done in praise of God. These verses emphasize the joy and dignity that can be found in our daily work and responsibilities.

O Thou Who Camest from Above

Jesus, confirm my heart's desire
   to work, and speak, and think for thee;
still let me guard the holy fire,
   and still stir up thy gift in me.

(Charles Wesley, 1707–88)

Brighten the Corner

Do not wait until some deed of greatness you may do,
do not wait to shed your light afar;
to the many duties ever near you now be true,
brighten the corner where you are.

Someone far from harbour you may guide across the bar;
brighten the corner where you are!

(Ina Duley Ogdon, b. 1877)

Ina Ogdon wrote these words in a fit of pique. She was
known as a talented speaker, and in 1913 was invited to
undertake a prestigious speaking tour when calamity

struck. Her father was involved in a car crash – and with great resentment, she agreed to cancel her tour in order to nurse him. Because she felt angry with God for allowing the tragedy to happen, she was bad-tempered with her father – until she stopped to think about how unkind she was being. She made a conscious decision to do whatever was needed in good heart to help her father recover, and be true to 'the many duties ever near'. Her words were teamed with a lilting melody, and the resulting hymn was chosen as the theme song for a major evangelical campaign in the States, which meant that her simple commitment of resolve and loving duty, although born out of disappointment and resentment, became dear to many.

A Touching Place

Feel for the people we most avoid.
Strange or bereaved or never employed;
feel for the women, and feel for the men
who fear that their living is all in vain.

To the lost Christ shows his face;
to the unloved he gives his embrace;
to those who cry in pain or disgrace,
Christ makes, with his friends, a touching place.

(John Bell and Graham Maule, b. 1949 and 1958)

However bad certain times in our lives may seem, they're unlikely to be as desperate as the people and situations described in this uncompromising hymn. I first heard it in Glasgow, which is where John Bell, a charismatic and inspirational worship leader of the Iona Community, has been based for years. That's a city in which he will have seen much sorrow, abuse and prejudice – and he's captured it all in these moving words, which challenge us to respond with compassion and Christian love to those whose lives are troubled. The everyday existence that John and his co-writer Graham describe may bear little resemblance to the comfortable, secure lives most of us lead – but this hymn spells out the painful experiences of many, and moves us to show fellowship however we can in ways that are practical and caring.

Brother, Sister, Let Me Serve You

We are pilgrims on a journey,
  and companions on the road;
we are here to help each other
  walk the mile and bear the load.

Brother, sister, let me serve you,
  let me be as Christ to you;
pray that I may have the grace to
  let you be my servant too.

(Richard Gillard, b. 1953)

Richard Gillard, who's a songwriter and worship leader in New Zealand, takes up the idea of pilgrimage in this much-loved hymn, which recognizes that whoever we are, whatever our talents or challenges, we're all human beings on the same walk of life. How much easier it would be if we could really think of everyone around us as fellow pilgrims and companions, helping one another to bear the load – less 'me', more 'we'!

But it's the last two lines that impress me the most. It's all too easy to be bountiful, bestowing your care on those you recognize are in need. It makes you feel good to give your service to others. It's much harder to accept *their* need to give too. Knowing how to *receive* with grace is also a gift you can give others, one that allows dignity and acknowledgement for both parties.

One More Step Along the World I Go

Give me courage when the world is rough,
keep me loving though the world is tough;
leap and sing in all I do,
keep me travelling along with you:

And it's from the old I travel to the new;
keep me travelling along with you.

(Sydney Carter, 1915–2004)

We're inclined to think of this as a children's song, but I think the deceptively simple language softens a meaningful message. It's adults who, with maturity, recognize just how tough the world can be, and how much courage and resilience may be needed simply to keep going. I have a suggestion though: when you're heading somewhere you really don't want to go, try singing these words and their jaunty melody to yourself. I always find they give me the confidence to keep on track!

Father, hear the prayer we offer:
not for ease that prayer shall be,
but for strength that we may ever
live our lives courageously.

(Love Maria Willis, 1824–1908)

Here's another prayer set to music that asks for strength and courage to cope with everything life brings our way. This was written by Love Maria Willis when she was still a young woman with her life uncharted before her – and perhaps it's the confidence of youth that has her reassuring God that she's not necessarily praying for an easy life ahead. As we grow older, we realize that life is seldom easy, and that strength and courage are exactly the qualities we need to cope with the challenges we come across. What we can do is to keep in mind God's promise that he won't ask us to cope with anything unless he knows we have the resources to deal with it – and sometimes we don't know how strong we can be until we *have* to cope with really hard times.

Day by day and with each passing moment,
strength I find to meet my trials here;
trusting in my Father's wise bestowment,
I've no cause for worry or for fear.
He whose heart is kind beyond all measure
gives unto each day what he deems best,
lovingly, its part of pain and pleasure,
mingling toil with peace and rest.

(Lina Sandell Berg, 1832–1903)

Hard times certainly spurred Swedish writer Lina Sandell Berg to write these words in 1858. She was with her father, a Lutheran minister, on board a ship crossing Lake Vattern in Gothenburg, when a sudden lurch catapulted her father into the sea where he drowned in front of her. This tragedy at first made her question how a loving God could allow such a thing to happen – and then turned her thoughts towards the need to trust God more than ever in heartbreaking circumstances like these. Such trust is never easy, and most of us would find her response hard to follow, but the promise of 'peace and rest' is very welcome when we too are struggling with tragic episodes in our lives.

Strong Son of God, Immortal Love

Our little systems have their day;
they have their day and cease to be;
they are but broken lights of thee,
and thou, O Lord, art more than they.

(Alfred, Lord Tennyson, 1809–92)

There are two hymns here that put into perspective the earthly things, either pleasurable or worrying, that occupy our time, alongside the lasting fulfilment of faith in God. The first, 'Strong Son of God', is by Alfred, Lord Tennyson who, as a rector's son, always understood the value of a good hymn. He wrote, 'In a good hymn you have to be both commonplace and poetical' – and, in typically poetic terms, this verse compares our 'little systems' with the omnipotence of God.

The poem 'I'd rather have Jesus', written by Rhea Miller, was left on a piano by the mother of a young George Beverly Shea, the American evangelist and singer – and the words challenged him so much that he immediately wrote the melody for this hymn, which became his theme tune as he went on to become a household favourite across America. Later he said, 'I never tire of Mrs Miller's heartfelt words', which he felt spurred him on to recognize what really mattered to him – to use his talents in God's service.

14

I'd rather have Jesus than silver or gold;
I'd rather be his than have riches untold;
I'd rather have Jesus than houses or land;
I'd rather be led by his nail-pierced hand.

I'd rather have Jesus than men's applause,
I'd rather be faithful to his dear cause;
I'd rather have Jesus than world-wide fame,
I'd rather be true to his holy name.

I'd rather have Jesus than anything
this world affords today.

(Rhea F. Miller, 1894–1966)

Lord, for the years your love has kept and guided,
urged and inspired us, cheered us on our way,
sought us and saved us, pardoned and provided,
Lord of the years, we bring our thanks today.

(Timothy Dudley-Smith, b. 1926)

Timothy Dudley-Smith is one of my favourite hymn writers,
mostly because he has the knack of capturing the essence of

our modern-day lives in poetry that resonates with love and praise of God. His hymn 'Lord, For the Years' has become a modern classic, now used at a variety of services of celebration or anniversary, which mark the passage of time. This is the verse I like most, especially for its image of God 'cheering us on our way'! When our daily lives seem to consist of more problems than pleasure, it's a lovely thought that God is keeping a watchful eye on us, encouraging us as we go. Timothy's words make us feel that we are individually special to God – and for that God is owed our thanks.

Benediction

> May God's blessing surround you each day,
> as you trust him and walk in his way.
> May his presence within
> guard and keep you from sin,
> go in peace, go in joy, go in love.

(Cliff Barrows, b. 1923)

Anyone who remembers Billy Graham's visits to the UK, Mission England (the last was in 1984), or perhaps owned a copy of the *Mission Praise* hymn book, will be very familiar with this Benediction, which was regularly sung by thousands at the end of huge events held at football stadiums around the country. Cliff Barrows became Dr Graham's Director of Music back in 1945, and over the years he was responsible for writing words and music to numerous favourites we all sing today. This hymn is dear to many because it's a simple, reassuring blessing to take you through every day of your life – and lovely words with which to say goodbye to someone you care about – 'go in peace, go in joy, go in love'.

O love that wilt not let me go

As human beings, there are certain essentials we need. Food, air, water and shelter are at the top of a very practical list, but because each one of us is a complex mix of heart, body and soul, it's not just practical needs that have to be answered. I believe the soul needs prayer as a constant connection to God – and our hearts have a deep-rooted necessity to reach out for love. A child created by and born into love has the best possible chance of growing to achieve all it could and should be. Without love, we feel lonely, rootless and worthless. Shown love, we then feel able to express our love for others – and it is that love which is the basis of family and community life. Love quite literally makes the world go round!

18

But in addition to our yearning for human love, there can be a gaping emptiness in our lives that can only be filled by the love of God, the Father who created us and supports each and every one of us in a personal and individual way. Some people choose to live in denial of that need – to assume that they are the instrument of their own destiny, and that the course of their lives, whether good or bad, will be only of their own making. Down the centuries, though, hymn writers have spoken from the heart about their experience of God, their wonder at the depth of his love, and their recognition of what that love means to them day by day.

George Matheson, a minister who had almost totally lost his sight by the time he was 18, was devastated when his fiancée jilted him just before their wedding because she didn't think she could face the prospect of being married to a blind man. That disappointment in human love seemed to spur him on to a greater appreciation of the unfailing love of God. He plainly suffered dark times, and it was during one such bout of depression that he wrote the lines of 'O Love That Wilt Not Let Me Go', which is one of the most evocative, plaintive and heartfelt of all hymns. There is infinite comfort in the words, 'O Love that wilt not let me go, I rest my weary soul in thee.' That is a love we can't help but long for!

O love that wilt not let me go,
　I rest my weary soul in thee;
I give thee back the life I owe,
that in thine ocean depths its flow
　may richer, fuller be.

O joy that seekest me through pain,
　I cannot close my heart to thee;
I trace the rainbow through the rain,
and feel the promise is not vain,
　that morn shall tearless be.

(George Matheson, 1842–1906)

Love divine, all loves excelling,
　joy of heaven, to earth come down,
fix in us thy humble dwelling,
　all thy faithful mercies crown.
Jesu, thou art all compassion,
　pure unbounded love thou art;
visit us with thy salvation,
　enter every trembling heart.

(Charles Wesley, 1707–88)

In the six thousand or so hymns he wrote, Charles Wesley returned again and again to the theme of his longing for God's love. His hymns often infuriated his brother, John, because Charles insisted on using intensely personal words like 'I' and 'my' in a way that was generally considered bad form in the eighteenth-century Church. But Charles was obviously a deeply emotional man whose passion for his faith flowed into his hymn writing. It was that passion that inspired him to write two or three hymns a day – because he simply couldn't stop praising, thanking and praying to be closer to the God he loved and longed to be loved by.

Charles Wesley's passionate words have stood the test of time, so that today they still speak to us and for us. We may envy his devotion and certainty, but most of all, we can't help but thank him for his ability to put into the most beautiful poetry the simple essence of the love we all long for.

> **O thou who camest from above**
>   the fire celestial to impart,
> kindle a flame of sacred love
>   on the mean altar of my heart!
>
> Ready for all thy perfect will,
>   my acts of faith and love repeat;
> till death thy endless mercies seal,
>   and make my sacrifice complete.

(Charles Wesley, 1707–88)

Just As I Am

Just as I am, thy love unknown
has broken every barrier down;
now to be thine, yea, thine alone,
O Lamb of God, I come.

Just as I am, of that free love
the breadth, length, depth and height to prove,
here for a season, then above,
O Lamb of God, I come.

(Charlotte Elliott, 1789–1871)

These beautiful, heartfelt lines were written back in 1834 by a delicate Victorian spinster, Charlotte Elliott, who made good use of the days when she was bed-bound by writing verses in praise of God. When she says she comes to God, 'just as I am', she aligns herself with all of us who sometimes feel inadequate because of our physical ability or mental weakness, personality or a sense of guilt for what we haven't or have done in the past. In Charlotte's case, ill health blighted her life from her early thirties until she died at the age of 82. Her feeling of uselessness and inadequacy was most acute when she was confined to bed at a time when the whole household was busily organizing a bazaar to raise funds for a much-needed school in Brighton where her brother was a minister. In desperation, she decided that her contribution would be to write a hymn – and what a hymn this turned out to be! Once it was published, not only did it finally raise much more in funds than anyone else's contribution, but it plainly tapped a vein of human experience which has endeared it to generations ever since.

Charlotte is a great example of the glorious fact that each of us has our own talents, which are unique and valuable. Our contribution may seem meagre compared with others, but the love with which we give carries much more worth than the size or status of the gift.

Such love, pure as the whitest snow;
such love weeps for the shame I know;
such love, paying the debt I owe;
O Jesus, such love.

Such love, stilling my restlessness;
such love, filling my emptiness;
such love, showing me holiness;
O Jesus, such love.

(Graham Kendrick, b. 1950)

Two centuries later, modern-day writer Graham Kendrick has also produced a very personal outpouring of his feeling of being an unworthy recipient of God's love. That divine love seems to make him complete, bringing with it calmness and fulfilment. He speaks of an 'emptiness' that many of us recognize from periods in our lives when we're disconnected from God – when prayers feel as if they're going nowhere, and we seem to be floundering alone. Often that feeling aligns with times when we're losing our way in our everyday lives, worrying that God wouldn't want to know us anyway! What Graham does in this hymn is reassure us that, in his experience, God can reach across that emptiness, filling the void with his love.

My song is love unknown,
my Saviour's love to me,
love to the loveless shown
that they might lovely be.
   O, who am I
   that for my sake
   my Lord should take
   frail flesh, and die?

O love that wilt not let me go

Here might I stay and sing:
no story so divine;
never was love, dear King,
never was grief like thine!
   This is my friend
   in whose sweet praise
   I all my days
   could gladly spend.

(Samuel Crossman, 1624–83)

In 1683, Samuel Crossman was buried in the south aisle of Bristol Cathedral where he'd been made Dean just a few months earlier after a lifetime of devotion as an Anglican clergyman. In his most famous hymn, 'My Song is Love Unknown', he also takes up the theme of inadequacy, expressing wonder that God should show such love 'to the loveless', which is how we all feel at the lowest points in our lives. But what I like most about this hymn is his acknowledgement of God as both king and friend, summing up in a few words his belief that the Lord with all his majesty is also accessible to us as a loving companion. I find that a very comforting thought – that a God omnipotent enough to create the heavens is also my friend who knows me, warts 'n' all, better than I know myself – and *still* loves me!

Another much younger hymn that takes up the theme of God being both king and friend is 'As the Deer Pants', written by Martyn Nystrom in the early 1980s. With the lilting melody that accompanies these words, this almost feels like a human love song, especially when it includes phrases like, 'You alone are my heart's desire' and, 'I love you more than any other'. Martyn has used the language of love to express his thanks to God for caring about each one of us in such a protective and comforting way.

As the Deer Pants

You're my friend and you are my brother,
even though you are a king,
I love you more than any other,
so much more than anything.

You alone are my strength, my shield,
to you alone may my spirit yield.
You alone are my heart's desire
and I long to worship you.

(Martyn Nystrom, b. 1956)

O love that wilt not let me go

When I survey the wondrous cross
 on which the Prince of glory died,
my richest gain I count but loss,
  and pour contempt on all my pride.

(Isaac Watts, 1674–1748)

Just as, today, it seems amazing to us that God should show unconditional love both universally and to us as individuals, so Isaac Watts was equally amazed 300 years ago! When it first appeared in 1707, 'When I Survey' was acknowledged as the first hymn ever to be written in the first person, with the pronoun 'I' expressing a personal experience of faith rather than simple doctrine.

Isaac Watts was a physically frail but intellectually brilliant and deeply emotional man, who longed for an intimate relationship with a loving God. He only ever wanted to express his innermost thoughts in the most personal and poetic way. For him, a few words could say so much – like the last two lines of this hymn, which humbly promise 'my soul, my life, my all' in response to the 'amazing love' of God. That's quite a promise! How many of us could pledge the same in our lives today?

27

Here is love vast as the ocean,
loving kindness as the flood,
when the Prince of life, our ransom,
shed for us his precious blood.
Who his love will not remember;
who can cease to sing his praise?
He can never be forgotten
throughout heaven's eternal days.

(Robert Lowry, 1826–99)

Here's another well-known hymn written on the other side of the Atlantic that marvels at God's endless love for us. Both words and music were written by Dr Robert Lowry, who was a popular Baptist minister in various churches on the east coast of North America, as well as being one of the most respected early gospel hymn writers. The secret of his popularity was almost certainly the beautiful simplicity of his words combined with easy-to-learn melodies that allowed congregations to sing at the top of their voices from the bottom of their hearts.

The last two lines about how God can never be forgotten always hit a note with me because I think we *do* forget God all too often. Our lives become so absorbing that it's easy to shunt thoughts about anything other than the nuts and bolts of life to the corner of our minds. The most surprising thing is that when we do eventually make time to remember God, he is still there – still patiently waiting, still giving and still loving us, in spite of our indifference to him.

Blessed Assurance

Perfect submission, all is at rest,
I in my Saviour am happy and blest –
watching and waiting, looking above,
filled with his goodness, lost in his love.

(Fanny J. Crosby, 1820–1915)

The blind gospel writer, Fanny Crosby, writing at the same time as Dr Lowry, would probably never have claimed to write 'beautiful' words, especially as she sometimes knocked out three hymns a day for various publishing houses who employed her. This wasn't just work, though. It was a mission which stemmed from her instinct to count her blessings rather than her limitations. There's a great joy throughout all of her hymns, and constant examples of her certainty that she was safe and cherished in the love of God. 'Lost in his love', she says in the last line of this verse. We all recognize the sense of being lost – but to be lost 'in his love'? What a wonderful feeling that would be! No wonder there's such joy in Fanny Crosby's hymns!

In heavenly love abiding,
    no change my heart shall fear;
and safe is such confiding,
    for nothing changes here:
the storm may roar without me,
    my heart may low be laid,
but God is round about me,
    and can I be dismayed?

(Anna Laetitia Waring, 1823–1910)

Just three years younger than Fanny Crosby, Anna Waring lived a very different life from her fellow hymn writer. She grew up in South Wales and was first a Quaker before later joining the Anglican Church. She dedicated much of her time to visiting prisoners in jail, which brought her face to face with desperate people in despairing circumstances. To them she took her ministry of a loving and forgiving God. How refreshing her words must have seemed to people who were feeling alone, forgotten and of little worth to anyone. She was able to reassure them that God would be alongside them during their darkest times, loving them even when they felt unlovable.

Make me a channel of your peace.
Where there is hatred, let me bring your love.
Where there is injury, your pardon, Lord,
and where there's doubt, true faith in you.

O Master, grant that I may never seek
so much to be consoled as to console,
to be understood as to understand,
to be loved, as to love with all my soul.

(Prayer of St Francis, 1181–1226, by Sebastian Temple,
1928–97)

There is a popular image of human beings as channels passing on to their neighbours the love they get from God. When writer Sebastian Temple was asked in 1967 to come up with both words and music for a collection of songs for the Franciscan Third Order's church in downtown Los Angeles, he used that idea of us as 'channels' for God's love as his interpretation of the first line of the famous prayer attributed to St Francis. What he created was a haunting melody to which humble words of service, fellowship and brotherly love are sung. These words are about giving in order to receive, listening rather than expecting to be listened to – but, most of all, loving so that we can be loved. There's an old saying, 'Love if you will be loved' – and that is so true. If you're feeling a bit unloved at the moment, perhaps you need to ask yourself how much love you are giving out. Are you being a 'channel' and passing on God's love to others?

O perfect love, all human thought transcending,
    lowly we kneel in prayer before your throne,
that theirs may be the love which knows no ending,
    who now for evermore are joined in one.

O perfect life, be now their full assurance
    of tender charity and steadfast faith,
of patient hope, and quiet brave endurance
    with childlike trust that fears not pain or death.

(Dorothy Frances Gurney, 1858–1932)

It's on family occasions like weddings and funerals that we find ourselves reaching for a hymn book to pick out just the right hymn to fit the moment. 'O Perfect Love', written around the 1900s, is the best I can think of for a marriage ceremony because by singing it the congregation are praying out loud for the qualities with which they hope the couple's life together will be blessed. This is a prayer set to music – fervent, hopeful and infinitely loving – a promise between the couple themselves, as well as a prayer from their friends and family who are there to support them as their two lives become one.

We Are One in the Spirit

We will work with each other, we will work side by side,
we will work with each other, we will work side by side,
and we'll guard each man's dignity and save each
    man's pride,
and they'll know we are Christians by our love,
    by our love,
yes, they'll know we are Christians by our love.

(Peter Scholtes, 1938–2009)

It's easy to talk sentimentally about love. It's much harder to apply it to needy people and situations. Surely, though, the proof of God's presence within our lives is our willingness to share his love with others. A life of love is a deliberate choice on our part, made in the face of our natural inclination to be self-centred. To live out our faith, to be a 'channel' for God's love on earth, is far harder than simply putting ourselves first, but in the end it is a more certain path to inner fulfilment.

Peter Scholtes's relatively modern hymn recalls the instruction in John 13.34 – 'As I have loved you, so you must love one another. By this all men will know that you are my disciples, if you love one another.' It's a good thought that as Christians we shouldn't be recognized by our uniforms, our protests or our demands – but simply by our love. Couldn't the world do with a lot more of that!

And Can It Be?

Amazing love! How can it be
that thou, my God, shouldst die for me?

(Charles Wesley, 1707–88)

It feels only right that the final thought on love should come from that most passionate lover of God, Charles Wesley.

These two lines from 'And Can It Be' must be among the most well-known and enthusiastically sung lines ever written. In little more than a dozen words he encapsulates the essence of our Christian faith. And, yes, it is amazing – because at the heart of it all is love, God's for us, and our loving gratitude to him!

Me comfort still

'Comfort' – it's hard to think of any word in the dictionary more heart-warming. It seems to carry so many other thoughts and emotions along with it – such as 'hug', 'closeness', 'safety', 'hiding place' and, most of all, 'loving'. It conjures up an image of being enclosed in the familiar embrace of your mum to whom you relinquish all your worries and hurts because you know she always makes things better. It's the feeling of being cosseted in big soft cushions with your feet up in front of your favourite TV programme – or waking in the night to hear rain battering your window when the clock says you still have hours to go before you need to surface. It's being replete after a delicious meal – or the sense of relief after a sneeze or a yawn! Comfort can dull sadness and suspend worry. It may not take practical problems away, but it certainly makes you feel better and stronger to deal with whatever faces you.

There are so many occasions in our lives when we long for spiritual comfort. In fact, can you think of any prayer you've ever breathed that didn't come from your hope that God might bless and bring comfort to challenging situations around you? This is particularly true in times of sadness or fear – when we're coping with bereavement, for example, or worried about illness, either our own or in someone we love. At those times, when we feel inadequate, unable to think of solutions or find the right words to provide comfort either to ourselves or to others, that's when we recognize that it's God's comfort we need. We know it may not stop the inevitable happening. It doesn't alter the sadness or pain we feel. We just long for the comfort of knowing that God is alongside us, his loving embrace a soothing balm to the pain we're going through.

God be with you till we meet again;
when life's perils thick confound you;
put his arms unfailing round you;
God be with you till we meet again.

(Jeremiah Eames Rankin, 1828–1904)

The words of this much-loved hymn never fail to bring a lump to the throat. Apparently it was sung by men leaving our shores to fight in the trenches of Flanders during the First World War. Tears spring to my own eyes as I remember that we chose it for the moment when the curtains closed in front of my mum's coffin during her funeral service. It speaks of parting and trepidation and sadness – but it is also infinitely loving and caring. How better to send a loved one on their way than by asking God to look after them when you can't be there to provide that comfort yourself?

When university president and congregational minister Jeremiah Rankin wrote these words in Washington DC in 1882, I wonder if he was prompted by his own concerns, perhaps because he was losing someone he loved? Whatever the reason, he created words that ever since have been a prayer on so many lips in times of trouble.

Another hymn often chosen for occasions when we're saying goodbye to our dearest loves is 'Be Still, My Soul', set to 'Finlandia', that glorious piece of music by Jean Sibelius, which was once described as sounding as if it had 'passed over black torrents and desolate moorlands, through pallid sunlight and grim primeval wet greys and blacks'. The verse I've chosen actually speaks of times 'when dearest friends depart and all is darkened in the vale of tears' – a graphic description of that frightening, helpless, pain-filled experience of bereavement and loss. Often the overriding sensation is one of fear – not for those who've gone because we know they are in a better place than the one of pain or illness that might have led to their death – but for ourselves, because so often bereavement leaves us feeling orphaned, left alone to cope in a world so much more bewildering and threatening without the strength and presence of that beloved person alongside us. These lines bring to mind the wise words of Psalm 46 – 'Be still, and know that I am God.' We can relax in that knowledge and, as the hymn says, allow God's love 'to soothe our sorrow, calm our fears', bringing the comfort and relief for which we long.

Be Still, My Soul

Be still, my soul: when dearest friends depart
   and all is darkened in the vale of tears,
then you shall better know his love, his heart,
   who comes to soothe your sorrow, calm your fears.
Be still, my soul: for Jesus can repay
from his own fullness all he takes away.

(Katharina von Schlegel, 1697–c.1768,
trans. Jane Borthwick, 1813–97)

Abide with me; fast falls the eventide;
the darkness deepens; Lord, with me abide!
When other helpers fail, and comforts flee,
help of the helpless, O abide with me.

(Henry Francis Lyte, 1793–1847)

Being left alone to cope with the loss of someone we love is a sad and challenging experience. Facing the fact that your own death is imminent is dreadful in a different way. As Christians, we believe that we are going to join our God. As human beings, the process of getting there fills us with dread and fear. We worry about the pain, the indignity, the complications, that might lead to our passing. On the whole, we don't fear death. What we dread is the act of dying.

It's no surprise that 'Abide With Me' is often chosen for funeral services, perhaps because Henry Francis Lyte was facing his own death as he wrote it. It's said that he penned these words in his study on the last evening he spent in the small fishing port of Lower Brixham in Devon, just after he'd preached a farewell sermon in the church where he'd been the minister for many years. The following day he sailed for Italy where, two months later, he died of consumption. His description of the 'darkness' around him in those last few weeks, the sense of being in the 'evening' of his life, creates an image we can easily picture – and his prayer that God should stay at his side while he feels 'helpless' seems to bring not only comfort, but reassurance too.

That other great hymn that speaks of walking 'through death's dark vale' takes its inspiration from perhaps the most well known of all the psalms. Comfort is etched in every line of these wonderful, ancient words, acknowledging our humanity and fear as we cope with the whole concept of death and dying. What strikes me most about this verse is its confidence, the absolute belief that however unnerving the journey, God is with us, a constant and comforting companion to share our fear and pain.

The Lord's My Shepherd

> Yea, though I walk through death's dark vale,
>   yet will I fear none ill;
> for thou art with me, and thy rod
>   and staff me comfort still.

(*The Scottish Psalter*, 1650)

Perhaps one of the reasons why we long for comfort as we approach the hard realities of life and death is because most

41

of us cherish our childhood memories of being comforted, probably by our parents, when we were too physically or emotionally immature to cope ourselves. Later in life, pain, frustrated physical effort or emotional turmoil can bring out in even the toughest and apparently most mature of us a deep longing to be drawn into a loving circle of care as reassuring and all-powerful as those childhood hugs. We remember how safe we felt when Mum, Dad, Nan or a big sister kissed our scraped knee better, told the bullies to go away or made us laugh when we woke in tears and terror after a bad dream. They took over, made the bad things go away and sorted all our problems out – and the child within us longs for that feeling throughout the length of our life.

More comforting still is the thought that Jesus said we need to be as trusting as small children if we are to enter the kingdom of heaven, so perhaps when we remember being embraced in love as children, we are in fact getting an idea of the character and infinite love of our God the Father.

Jesus loves me! This I know,
for the Bible tells me so.
Little ones to him belong;
they are weak, but he is strong.

(Anna Bartlett Warner, 1820–1915)

42

Anna Bartlett Warner and her sister Susan were talented sisters who lived most of their lives in a large mansion on Constitution Island in the Hudson River. Every Sunday afternoon, cadets from West Point Military Academy were rowed over to the island by a servant so that they could take part in Bible classes run by the pair, followed by tea and gingerbread. Both sisters were highly successful and popular writers, and it was in Anna's novel *Say and Seal* (written under her pseudonym, Amy Lothrop) that the words of this hymn were said at the bedside of a dying little boy. Since then, 'Jesus Loves Me' has become a favourite for children around the world, often learned at Sunday school. The key to its popularity might be the simplicity of its message or the familiar lilting melody – but I think the main reason why these words remain steadfastly in our minds is the reassurance of Christ's loving strength throughout the times in our lives when we feel inadequate, weak and childlike.

'Tell Me the Old, Old Story' is another hymn often remembered from Sunday school days. It reminds us of the reassurance most of us felt within our family circle, and our unquestioning acceptance that God was good, loving and all-powerful. There may have been a 'cosiness' in our image of God then, an understanding of him that needed to mature through the ups and downs of life. What Arabella 'Kate' Hankey, who taught Sunday school in Croydon more than a century ago, captures in these words is a belief that although our first introduction to the gospel may have come when our understanding was childish and simplistic, the truth of God's presence throughout our lives remains constant. This became real to her when, at the age of 30, she went through a serious illness. She wrote then that 'simple thoughts in simple words are all we can bear in sickness'. Hers must have been a long illness because originally she wrote 50 verses – although only eight are regularly sung now!

Tell Me the Old, Old Story

Tell me the story simply,
as to a little child,
for I am weak and weary,
and helpless and defiled.

Tell me the story always,
if you would really be,
in any time of trouble
a comforter to me.

(Arabella Katherine Hankey, 1834–1911)

Take the name of Jesus with you,
child of sorrow and of woe,
it will joy and comfort give you;
take it then, where'er you go.

(Lydia Baxter, 1809–74)

Lydia Baxter knew a great deal about 'sorrow and woe' because as an invalid she was bedridden for most of her life. Although she was described as always cheerful and patient, there must have been times when the limitations of her situation frustrated and depressed her, especially as her illness worsened. 'Take the Name of Jesus With You' was written just four years before her death at the age of 65. Around that time she told a friend, 'I have a very special armour. I have the name of Jesus. When the tempter tries to make me blue or despondent, I mention the name of Jesus, and he can't get through to me any more.' The Christ she was taught about in her childhood remained a constant friend throughout her life – good advice for any of us!

O Worship the Lord in the Beauty of Holiness

Low at his feet lay thy burden of carefulness:
   high on his heart he will bear it for thee,
comfort thy sorrows, and answer thy prayerfulness,
   guiding thy steps as may best for thee be.

(John Samuel Bewley Monsell, 1811–75)

Just as the previous hymn advised us to 'take Jesus with us', so John Monsell suggests that as we go through life we should lay down our burdens of care and sorrow in prayer to Christ, and allow him to comfort and guide us as we move onwards. John Monsell also wrote that old favourite, 'Fight the Good Fight' – and sometimes getting through difficult times can feel like a bit of a battle! These words, though, reassure us that whenever we feel battered by the challenges of life, God's comfort is there for us as we seek it in prayer.

I need thee every hour,
most gracious Lord.
No tender voice like thine
can peace afford.

I need thee, O I need thee!
Every hour I need thee!
O bless me now, my Saviour,
I come to thee.

(Annie Sherwood Hawks, 1835–1918)

These words came to Annie Hawks when she was a 37-year-old housewife going about her regular tasks. She became filled with a sense of nearness to God, wondering how anyone could live without him, whether in joy or in pain. The hymn that formed in her mind soon became hugely popular, in a way that she didn't truly understand until 16 years later, when she described herself as being 'in the shadow of a great loss' after the death of her husband. It was then that she experienced for herself 'something of the comforting power in the words' that 'had touched the throbbing heart of humanity'.

'Throbbing' is a good word to describe the awful pain of grief. It reminds you of how dreadful you feel with relentless tooth or ear ache, when medication brings scant relief. In Annie's own experience, the only possible relief in the face of the throbbing pain of grief was the comfort that God's nearness alone can bring.

Come down, O Love divine,
   seek thou this soul of mine,
and visit it with thine own ardour glowing;
   O Comforter, draw near,
   within my heart appear,
and kindle it, thy holy flame bestowing.

(Bianco da Siena, 1350–1434, trans. Richard F. Littledale, 1833–90)

For centuries, the Holy Spirit has often been described as 'the Comforter' who brings peace and healing to troubled hearts and minds. 'Come Down, O Love Divine' is one of the best-known hymns to pick up this theme. Although it is very much a modern favourite, the words date back to a poem originally written in Italian in the fourteenth century by Bianco da Siena, who began his working life as an apprentice in the wool trade in Tuscany before joining an order of mystics when he was just seventeen. He'd probably moved to Venice by the time he wrote these reassuring words. Later, the ancient manuscript was rediscovered and published. This translation of four of the verses was made by Dr Littledale, a scholarly man who studied and translated many Latin and Greek inspirational works.

Writing around the same time as Dr Littledale, American Methodist minister Frank Bottome dedicated a whole hymn to the traditional idea of the Holy Spirit as the Comforter, bringing solace and peace to hearts and souls that are weighed down with sadness and pain.

The Comforter Has Come

O spread the tidings round wherever man is found,
wherever human hearts and human woes abound;
let every Christian tongue proclaim the joyful sound:
the Comforter has come!

(Frank Bottome, 1823–94)

O Sacred Head, Sore Wounded

I pray thee, Jesus, own me,
  me, Shepherd good, for thine;
who to thy fold hast won me,
  and fed with truth divine.

Me guilty, me refuse not,
 incline thy face to me,
this comfort that I lose not,
 on earth to comfort thee.

(Robert Bridges, 1844–1930)

'O Sacred Head, Sore Wounded' is another hymn popular today that has its roots in ancient words – in this case the long medieval poem, *Salve mundi salutare*, which was originally written in Latin. The powerful Passiontide poem addresses in turn the various parts of Christ's body hanging on the cross, and the last verses, from which these words are taken, invoke the Saviour's head. The beauty of the plea for God's care and comfort shines through these ancient words, which were translated from the original Latin many times over the years. The verse I have chosen here comes from the translation made at the end of the nineteenth century by Robert Bridges.

In Christ alone my hope is found;
he is my light, my strength, my song;
this cornerstone, this solid ground,
firm through the fiercest drought and storm.

> What heights of love, what depths of peace,
> when fears are stilled, when strivings cease!
> My comforter, my all in all –
> here in the love of Christ I stand.
>
> (Stuart Townend and Keith Getty)

The song-writing team of Stuart Townend and Keith Getty have drawn together so many elements of the comfort of God's presence in this hymn, 'In Christ Alone'. Set to a lilting Irish melody, the incisive words touch raw nerves and provide encouragement to Christians of all ages and backgrounds.

One young soldier wrote to say he'd sung 'In Christ alone' to himself almost every night while on war-zone duty. 'We are losing soldiers here every day,' he wrote, 'to people that we are trying to help. To know that Christ purposefully gave His life for us helps me to understand that He knows that soldiers are dying and that He is in control.' He went on to say how comforted he was by that thought, which made him feel more secure than the M-16 he carried or the 9mm pistol tucked in his flak jacket pocket – and when bullets are flying and comrades are falling around you, that must be comfort indeed!

Lead us, heavenly Father, lead us

If we think of our lives as a journey, it can sometimes feel as if we face a route full of unexpected turns, uphill climbs and hidden pitfalls – not to mention the fact that we seem to spend a lot of time in the dark! The fact that we never quite know what's round the corner can be one of life's pleasures – but there's a fine line between that and the feeling of uncertainty and vulnerability that comes when we lack direction or control over what lies ahead. It's not surprising, then, that hymn writers down the years, as well as recognizing and giving thanks for where God's guidance has already brought them, have responded to that feeling of being lost and alone by writing hymns that express a longing for guidance from a loving, caring, all-seeing God.

Perhaps the most famous and best loved of all hymns

asking for God's guidance is the wonderful 'Guide Me, O Thou Great Jehovah'. The words were written by a man who often needed guidance in a very practical way. William Williams was a young Welshman whose life was turned upside down when by chance he heard the controversial preacher Howell Harris talking to a crowd in a churchyard. William was fired with commitment and when, years later, his outspoken views led to his being turned down for ministry in the Anglican Church, he followed the example of Howell Harris and became an itinerant preacher.

William Williams travelled over one hundred thousand miles by foot and on horseback, often being welcomed by enthusiastic crowds, but sometimes being turned away with sticks and insults. In those days, before accurate maps and satnav, imagine how difficult it must have been to know how long each journey would take, or in which direction to head out! I guess this plea for guidance was sometimes as much for his aching feet as for his flagging soul!

> **Guide me, O thou great Jehovah,**
>   pilgrim through this barren land;
> I am weak, but thou art mighty;
>   hold me with thy powerful hand:
>   Bread of heaven, bread of heaven,
>   feed me now and evermore.

(William Williams, 1717–91, trans. Peter Williams, 1727–96)

Thy hand, O God, has guided
  thy flock, from age to age;
the wondrous tale is written,
  full clear on every page;
our fathers owned thy goodness,
  and we their deeds record;
and both of this bear witness:
  one church, one faith, one Lord.

(Edward Hayes Plumptre, 1821–91)

This stirring hymn from Edward Hayes Plumptre is often sung during services that mark the passing of time, like anniversaries and ceremonies of remembrance. 'Thy Hand, O God, Has Guided' recognizes God's part, not just in our lives, but in every generation before us. There is something deeply comforting in looking back and seeing that however desperate people may have felt during challenging times in their lives, the testimony of history shows that things often worked out in ways that eventually were for the best. It reassures us that God can see a much bigger picture of us and our place in the world than we can ever imagine.

As with gladness men of old
did the guiding star behold,
as with joy they hailed its light,
leading onward, beaming bright;
so, most gracious Lord, may we
evermore be led to thee.

(William Chatterton Dix, 1837–98)

Probably the most memorable example of God's guidance in the Bible is found in the story of the Epiphany, when the three wise men followed a star that guided them to where the infant Jesus lay. It was that image which moved William Chatterton Dix to write the much-loved Christmas carol, 'As with Gladness'. William's life was dogged by illness, and when, in his early twenties, he wrote these now famous words, he was laid up in bed, probably feeling very low. In spite of his malaise, this is a hymn that resounds with joy and hope – qualities that he must have longed for at times when illness brought him down, both physically and spiritually.

Jesus, Good Above All Other

Lord, in all our doings guide us;
pride and hate shall ne'er divide us;
we'll go on with thee beside us,
    and with joy, we'll persevere.

(Percy Dearmer, 1867–1936)

Joy is also the overriding sentiment of this verse from 'Jesus, Good Above All Other', a hymn I remember with great affection from my junior school days. Percy Dearmer was a leading light in a small committee formed in 1906 to produce *The English Hymnal*, described as 'a collection of the best hymns in the English language'. Luminaries such as Ralph Vaughan Williams and Gustav Holst were brought in to help pair music with words – with Percy acting mostly as text editor although, as this hymn shows, he also contributed words himself.

The charm of this hymn is its simplicity, which makes it suitable even for children – like me as a youngster! Standing in assembly in school uniform and short socks singing, 'We'll go on with thee beside us' – now, that's not only a memory that's hard to forget, but an intention that has stayed with me ever since!

There is no moment of my life,
no place where I may go,
no action which God does not see,
no thought he does not know.
Before I speak, my words are known,
and all that I decide.
To come or go: God knows my choice,
and makes himself my guide.

(Brian Foley, 1919–2000)

Brian Foley's 'There is No Moment' continues the thought that throughout our journey of everyday life, God is at our side. More than that, Brian suggests that we go nowhere, do nothing, think no thought of our own without God knowing it first. It acknowledges that we do have choice, but because God knows each of us so well, that choice is known to him before we even realize there's a decision to be made. What's more, whatever choice we make, even if it's a bad one, God remains by our side as our guide.

That's not an original thought because way back in the early fifth century, St Patrick was putting into words something very similar in his famous text 'St Patrick's Breastplate', from which the words below are taken. You can almost sense the relief in his heartfelt belief that he is protected in every way by God's wisdom and power and his constant presence, which listens, holds and leads us through our journey of life.

I bind unto myself today
the power of God to hold and lead,
his eye to watch, his might to stay,
his ear to hearken to my need.
The wisdom of my God to teach,
his hand to guide, his shield to ward;
the word of God to give me speech,
his heavenly host to be my guard.

(St Patrick, 372–466, trans. Cecil Frances Alexander,
1818–95)

Father, I place into your hands
the things I cannot do.
Father, I place into your hands
the times that I've been through.
Father, I place into your hands
the way that I should go,
for I know I always can trust you.

(Jenny Hewer, b. 1945)

The simple, everyday language of this modern hymn by
Jenny Hewer is touching and relevant to situations in which

we all find ourselves at times. How often do you feel defeated by your lack of ability or opportunity to put wrongs right, get cracking with something you have to achieve or move on to a goal you desperately want to reach? How wonderful to be able to lay all the obstacles and your frustration in God's hands, trusting that he will support you through it! That doesn't mean you'll get everything you pray for, because part of that trust is recognizing that God sees a bigger picture than you can imagine, and that what's best in the long run is his will rather than your wishes. That can be hard to accept – but probably not as hard as that feeling of banging your head against a brick wall when you are constantly frustrated by what you can't quite manage to achieve in your own strength.

All the way my Saviour leads me,
what have I to ask beside?
Can I doubt His tender mercy,
who through life has been my guide?
Heavenly peace, divinest comfort,
here by faith in him to dwell!
For I know whate'er befall me,
Jesus doeth all things well.

(Fanny J. Crosby, 1820–1915)

59

When Queen Victoria was on the throne in Britain, Fanny Crosby was making a name for herself in the States by writing hymn texts. She wrote about eight thousand, sometimes two or three in one day! She died at the age of 95, having endured a life of constant challenge, yet she wrote of being thankful and joyful just to be alive! At the age of just a few weeks she lost her sight in a tragic accident when she was given the wrong medical treatment. A sightless person is keenly aware of stumbling and uncertainty, so she knew all too well the importance of guided steps, as we see in this hymn.

Life was never easy. One day when she desperately needed five dollars but had no idea how she could get it, she did what she always did. She prayed about it! Minutes later a stranger appeared at her door with the exact amount of money she needed. 'I have no way of accounting for this,' she said, 'except to believe that God put it into the heart of this good man to bring the money. My first thought was that it is so wonderful the way the Lord leads me, I immediately wrote the poem.' She went on to say that it reminded her that God has never promised to keep us from hard places or exhaustion in life, but has assured us that he will go with us, guide each step and give us grace. What a reassuring thought that is when we are feeling lost and exhausted by life!

Jesus, Saviour, pilot me
over life's tempestuous sea;
unknown waves before me roll,
hiding rocks and treach'rous shoal;
chart and compass come from thee –
Jesus, Saviour, pilot me!

(Edward Hopper, 1818–88)

'Tempestuous' – that's a grand old word, and one that appears in both this hymn and the next, which liken our journey through life to a ship battling across a stormy sea. Just as a ship's captain relies on both his instruments and his instincts to lead him through, so these hymns ask for God's guidance to protect, lead and bring us safely home. The words 'Jesus, Saviour, pilot me' would have spoken volumes to Edward Hopper's nineteenth-century congregation at the Church of the Sea and Land in New York Harbour.

Across the Atlantic at more or less the same time, James Edmeston was painting a similar image for the children of the London Orphan Asylum, for whom he wrote hymn texts almost every week. For these youngsters, who lived far from the sea, the idea of God guiding their way through life's storms must have seemed rather exciting and romantic!

Lead us, heavenly Father, lead us
　o'er the world's tempestuous sea;
guard us, guide us, keep us, feed us,
　for we have no help but thee;
yet possessing every blessing,
　if our God our Father be.

(James Edmeston, 1791–1867)

Holy Spirit, faithful guide,
ever near the Christian's side,
gently lead us by the hand,
pilgrims in a desert land;
weary souls fore'er rejoice,
while they hear that sweetest voice
whispering softly, 'Wanderer come!
Follow me, I'll guide thee home.'

(Marcus M. Wells, 1815–95)

Far from the high seas, these next two hymns picture us as pilgrims in the desert, alone, weak and frightened. The bleakness of the landscape is graphic and threatening, but that's balanced by our sense of pilgrimage as we make our way through our journey of life and faith. Out of that image come these two hymns which tell of God leading us on with strength and certainty.

Farmer Marcus Wells came up with the idea for the words of 'Holy Spirit, Faithful Guide' as he worked on a hot day in his cornfield near Hardwick, New York. Bob Dufford, on the other hand, is a Jesuit who may not have had a similar experience – the barren desert he speaks of is spiritual rather than actual. It recalls the forty days and nights that Jesus spent in the desert when he was taunted and tempted by the devil. There are times in our own lives when we feel we're in a spiritual wasteland, thirsting for inspiration and guidance. Bob Dufford's reassuring lines affirm that however lost we may feel, God is always at our side – and that true rest will be our reward at the end of the journey.

> **You shall cross the barren desert,**
> but you shall not die of thirst.
> You shall wander far in safety
> though you do not know the way.
> You shall speak your words in foreign lands
> and all will understand.
> You shall see the face of God and live.
>
> *Be not afraid. I go before you always.*
> *Come, follow me, and I will give you rest.*

(Bob Dufford, b. 1943)

Spirit of God, Unseen as the Wind

Without your help we fail our Lord,
we cannot live his way;
we need your power, we need your strength,
following Christ each day.

(Margaret Old, b. 1932)

Margaret Old spent thirty years as an editor for Scripture Union where she combined a passion for reaching young people with the Christian message through Sunday school teaching with the production of educational and inspirational books to help those working with children. She chose to write new words for the famous 'Skye Boat Song', creating a much-loved hymn that recognizes our need of God in order to be strong enough to 'live his way' in our daily lives.

O Jesus, I Have Promised

O let me see thy footmarks,
    and in them plant mine own;
my hope to follow duly
    is in thy strength alone.

O guide me, call me, draw me,
  uphold me to the end;
and then in heaven receive me,
  my Saviour and my Friend.

(John E. Bode, 1816–74)

Wanting to follow Christ, although not actually knowing how to do that in the muddle of our modern living, can prove quite a challenge. Here are two hymns that ask for guidance in the simplest way – that we should be able to see where Christ is leading us and follow in his footsteps. The Reverend John Bode wrote 'O Jesus, I Have Promised' for the confirmation services of his own three children because he thought they would be helped by this very clear illustration of God's guidance.

Jane Leeson also had children in mind when she wrote the next hymn, which imagines Jesus as a shepherd gathering his flock behind him as he leads them safely along the narrow path home. This hymn has all the reassurance of a parent firmly holding a child's hand as they travel together. The child is totally trusting, and it is that childlike trust that we need. In spite of the difficulties facing us, and our own ideas of how we might sort things out, these hymns suggest that if we trust Christ without question, he will bring us safely through.

Loving Shepherd of Your Sheep

Loving Shepherd ever near,
teach your lamb your voice to hear;
let my footsteps never stray
from the straight and narrow way.

(Jane E. Leeson, 1808–81)

Lead, kindly light, amid the encircling gloom,
    lead thou me on;
the night is dark, and I am far from home,
    lead thou me on.
Keep thou my feet; I do not ask to see
the distant scene; one step enough for me.

(John Henry Newman, 1801–90)

When John Newman wrote the long piece of devotional
poetry from which 'Lead, Kindly Light' comes, he was feeling physically exhausted and intellectually bewildered by
the first stirring of doubts which were to take him, 15 years
later, into the Roman Catholic Church. He was searching
for truth and certain belief, but the path to that felt dark

and uncharted, which is why he cried out from the depths of his soul for God to lead him home. This most human of reactions is one we might not expect from someone as stoical as Queen Victoria, but it's said she asked for the words of this hymn to be read out to her as she lay dying at Osborne House on the Isle of Wight in January 1901.

Abide With Me

I need thy presence every passing hour;
what but thy grace can foil the tempter's power?
Who like thyself my guide and stay can be?
Through cloud and sunshine, O abide with me.

(Henry Francis Lyte, 1793–1847)

Guidance is never more passionately longed for than in the dark times of our lives when we feel lost, threatened and very alone. Here we have two hymns that capture that feeling of uncertainty and aloneness, both of which are all the more poignant when sung to their familiar haunting melodies.

The idea of going home is one that often comes into the minds of mourners when someone they love has died, which is why 'Abide With Me', written by Henry Francis Lyte when he was well aware he hadn't long to live, is such a popular choice during funeral services. The ultimate step into the unknown is death itself, and our instinctive wish is that, although we approach our going with trepidation and fear, we will be guided 'home' and welcomed. This verse, asking for God not only to stay with us as we approach death, but also to be our guide because we need his presence then more than ever, puts into beautiful poetry the longing every human feels at this most vulnerable time in their lives.

When Sir Henry Williams Baker wrote his paraphrase of Psalm 23 in 'The King of Love My Shepherd Is', he too pictured the fear-filled darkness during that part of our life's journey which takes us to our death. Like the psalmist three thousand years ago, he realizes that our fear can only be answered by God's comfort and guidance.

The King of Love My Shepherd Is

In death's dark vale I fear no ill
　　with thee, dear Lord, beside me;
thy rod and staff my comfort still,
　　thy cross before to guide me.

(Henry Williams Baker, 1821–77)

O God, our help in ages past,
    our hope for years to come,
be thou our guide while life shall last,
    and our eternal home.

(Isaac Watts, 1674–1748)

This triumphant hymn by Isaac Watts is often chosen for remembrance services, or any other event that recognizes the trials we've faced in the past, and our need of God's guidance and protection in the future. This glorious hymn with its reassuring words sounds wonderful as it echoes around a great cathedral. It has me not only believing every word, but has the hairs on the back of my neck standing bolt upright! Great stuff!

Forgive our foolish ways

The prayer Jesus taught us to say each day contains lines that seem to me to be right at the heart of our relationship with God: 'Forgive us our sins as we forgive those who sin against us.'

As Christians, we believe that Christ died for our sins so that we can be forgiven. We say the Lord's Prayer in faith – and surely faith and forgiveness are like right and left hand to each other. We ask God for forgiveness in faith that we will be heard, and because we feel God has heard and recognized our genuine desire to acknowledge our sins, we accept his faithfulness in forgiving us.

God knows we fail so often and in so many ways. We know that too. In our Eucharist services, we ask God to forgive us because 'we have sinned against you and against our fellow men in thought and word and deed'. We can never say any of these words without some very specific failing creeping into our mind and conscience. Often our 'sins' are not what we do, but what we omit to do – like not showing kindness and compassion when we could, or putting our own needs first because that's easier than being patient and thoughtful to others.

Sometimes, though, our sins are much easier to identify because they involve an action on our part that is blatantly unfair, negligent or hurtful to someone else. On other occasions, it is our reaction that becomes a sin – for example, when we are the victims of a hurt or injury, as a result of which we feel resentful and long for revenge.

I can't count the number of times during *Songs of Praise* interviews when people have talked about what a relief it's been for them to let go of long-held anger and allow themselves to forgive. I remember most graphically the story told me by an old soldier who had suffered terribly as a Japanese prisoner of war during the Second World War. He talked of how, four decades later, he had travelled back with a group of his fellow prisoners to the town in which the prison camp had been. What he found there was welcome and genuine regret for the suffering the prisoners had gone through during the war years – and the heartfelt need for forgiveness felt by that next generation of Japanese towns-people softened his heart. He later described his hatred and longing for revenge as a cancer that had been festering inside him for years. 'I will never be able to forget,' he said, 'but I know I must forgive.'

Our spirit is tattered by resentment, regret, anger and omission. We suffer for it with feelings of depression, anxiety, unhappiness, hopelessness and despair. That is why we need forgiveness. We have to forgive those who have hurt us – and ask for forgiveness for all the hurt we ourselves have caused others. Bitterness and an inability to forgive are barriers to true faith. Surely, we can best show our faith in God by forgiving those who have let us down – just as he forgives us on all the many occasions when we fail him.

Dear Lord and Father of mankind,
   forgive our foolish ways;
re-clothe us in our rightful mind,
in purer lives thy service find,
   in deeper reverence praise,
   in deeper reverence praise.

Breathe through the heats of our desire
   thy coolness and thy balm;
let sense be dumb, let flesh retire;
speak through the earthquake, wind and fire,

O still small voice of calm,
O still small voice of calm!

(John Greenleaf Whittier, 1807–92)

This hymn is constantly voted a favourite by *Songs of Praise* viewers – partly, I'm sure, because the combination of John Greenleaf Whittier's beautiful poetry and 'Repton', the soaring melody by Sir Hubert Parry, creates a perfect partnership, providing congregations with a vehicle for worship that lifts heart and soul. More than that, every line of this hymn seems to hit the spot, touching raw nerves, guilty consciences and homing in on our longing to be at peace with God.

I'm sure you're familiar with the very last verse, which talks about God's 'still small voice of calm' bringing 'coolness and balm'. When we're struggling with the burden of our own wrongdoing, or with resentment about what we feel are the failings of others, the idea of God's forgiveness bringing 'coolness and balm' sounds wonderful – like a long, cold drink to a throat that is parched and thirsty.

'Forgive our sins, as we forgive',
   you taught us, Lord, to pray;
but you alone can grant us grace
   to live the words we say.

How can your pardon reach and bless
   the unforgiving heart
that broods on wrongs, and will not let
   old bitterness depart?

(Rosamond Herklots, 1905–87, based on Matthew 6.12)

This twentieth-century hymn by Rosamond Herklots expresses the feeling of human inadequacy most of us recognize when we think about trying to live out those words, 'Forgive our sins as we forgive.' The stumbling block often comes when we stew over the wrongs in our lives that we just can't seem to get over – those hurts and slights for which, however much we try not to, we find ourselves harbouring resentment or perhaps even a wish for revenge. It's relatively easy to ask for God's forgiveness for our own sins. It seems much harder to forgive others who sin against us – and the frustration is that that's a sin too! It does give us real understanding, though, of the depth of God's love for us – that even when we feel we are beyond forgiveness, we are met by welcome, understanding and acceptance.

Brian Foley takes up the same theme of forgiveness in his hymn, 'How Can We Sing With Joy to God', although these verses relate less to our need to forgive others, and more to our own faults, which fall short of what we'd like to be. Brian even goes so far as to describe our lives as godless – because when we put our own wants and desires in front of our care for others, we do become detached from God in a very real way. It's all too easy to ignore any thoughts of Christian principles when we really just want to do our own thing with little consideration for anyone but ourselves. But however distant we may become from God, he remains close to us – close enough to see our mistakes and faults, but closer still in His patience and forgiveness.

> **How can we sing with joy to God,**
> how can we pray to him,
> when we are far away from God
> in selfishness and sin?
>
> God knows the sinful things we do,
> the godless life we live,
> yet in his love he calls to us,
> so ready to forgive.

(Brian Foley, 1919–2000)

Take This Moment, Sign and Space

Take the time to call my name,
take the time to mend
who I am and what I've been,
all I've failed to tend.

Take the tiredness of my days,
take my past regret;
letting your forgiveness touch
all I can't forget.

(John Bell and Graham Maule, b. 1949 and 1958)

John Bell and Graham Maule of the Iona Community always manage to weave into their hymns the threads of everyday life. The picture they paint is rarely rosy. Their words are full of realism and humanity. They take human beings as nowadays they so often are – inadequate, weary, stumbling and fearful – and yet what they write is never hurtful or criticizing, simply touching and incisive. When we sing 'Take This Moment', we all recognize that feeling of tiredness and regret, and are aware of ways in which we've failed to come up to scratch – but God is able to acknowledge it all, and still meet us with forgiveness.

Just As I Am

Just as I am, thou wilt receive,
wilt welcome, pardon, cleanse, relieve:
because thy promise I believe,
  O Lamb of God, I come.

(Charlotte Elliott, 1789–1871)

Writing nearly two centuries ago, Charlotte Elliott recognized that same of sense of being unworthy of God's love and forgiveness. The hymn she wrote expressing that feeling, 'Just As I Am', has spoken right to the heart of people ever since. She knew that she needed to be 'pardoned, cleansed and relieved' because of all she felt she lacked, and yet she speaks of coming to Christ 'just as I am'. She learned to accept her own failures – in other words, to forgive herself. Perhaps forgiving ourselves – letting ourselves off the hook of our own condemnation – is the first step we must take in order to experience the forgiveness of God.

In her hymn, Charlotte Elliott writes of being received by Christ 'just as I am' – but the reality is that if we are burdened down by a feeling of failure and shortcoming, then we don't expect God to *want* to receive us. And because the Bible speaks not only of a loving, forgiving God, but also of his judgement, who can blame us for being fearful about his reaction?

William Cowper was a man who worried a lot about everything. He was a manic depressive, who at one time tried to commit suicide, and whose life was dogged by melancholy and self doubt. It was when he met John Newton, the former slave-trader-turned-minister in Olney in Buckinghamshire, that he found more peace both within himself and with God. God's judgement didn't seem so damning then – and Cowper was able to write with wonder and confidence about the limitations of our understanding. The image he conjures up of God apparently having a 'frowning providence' behind which he 'hides a smiling face' is warmly reassuring.

God Moves in a Mysterious Way

Judge not the Lord by feeble sense,
    but trust him for his grace;
behind a frowning providence
    he hides a smiling face.

(William Cowper, 1731–1800)

Because He Lives

God sent his son, they called him Jesus;
he came to love, heal and forgive;
he lived and died to buy my pardon,
an empty grave is there to prove my Saviour lives.

Because I know he holds the future,
and life is worth the living just because he lives.

(Gloria and William Gaither, b. 1942 and 1936)

Gloria and William Gaither, who are well-known American worship leaders, wrote this hymn at a time of great uncertainty not just for them as a couple, but for the world as a whole. It was at the end of the sixties, when the United States was going through great turmoil, with the Vietnam War claiming the lives of thousands of young people and many others falling into a sinister drug and alcohol culture. At that time, Gloria found she was expecting a baby, and the couple struggled over the wisdom of bringing a child into such a world. However, when baby Benjy finally did arrive, they were overcome by a sense of God's love, and his reassurance that the sins of the world could find forgiveness and loving welcome in him. It led Gloria to feel that 'this child can face uncertain days because Christ lives'.

And Can It Be?

Long my imprisoned spirit lay
    fast bound in sin and nature's night:
thine eye diffused a quickening ray;
    I woke, the dungeon flamed with light;
my chains fell off, my heart was free,
I rose, went forth and followed thee.

(Charles Wesley, 1707–88)

These next two hymns resound with the profound joy and relief that come from receiving God's forgiveness. The image Charles Wesley paints of his spirit being imprisoned in a dark dungeon by sin, until the cell is suddenly filled with light, his chains fall off and his heart is free, is one of the most graphic and stirring I can think of in any hymn! When you stand in a large congregation singing those last two lines with volume and conviction, it feels intensely personal and re-affirming.

In 'Great is Thy Faithfulness', Thomas Chisholm talks not so much about the freedom forgiveness brings but the lasting peace, strength and hope that come through pardon from sin. More than that, he sees new mercies every morning. It does seem that at those times when we're thinking more about ourselves than anyone else, we can be so self-absorbed that we become blind to the blessings around us.

Once we ask for forgiveness and are more in fellowship with God, that's when we begin to recognize the many gifts we've been given within ourselves, and in the people and surroundings we love.

Great is Thy Faithfulness

Pardon for sin and a peace that endureth,
    thine own dear presence to cheer and to guide;
strength for today and bright hope for tomorrow,
    blessings all mine, with ten thousand beside!

Great is thy faithfulness! Great is thy faithfulness!
Morning by morning new mercies I see;
all I have needed thy hand hath provided,
Great is thy faithfulness, Lord, unto me.

(Words: Thomas O. Chisholm, 1866–1960. © 1923, ren. 1951,
Hope Publishing Co., Carol Stream, IL 60188.)

Make Me a Blessing

Tell the sweet story of Christ and his love.
Tell of his power to forgive;
others will trust him if only you prove
true every moment you live.

(Ira B. Wilson, 1880–1950)

The words of this hymn, 'Make Me a Blessing', paint a simple picture because they were written primarily with children in mind. In fact, 1,000 copies of the song were printed in 1924 for a Sunday school convention in Cleveland, Ohio, where it was received with such enthusiasm that it soon became popular far and wide. The theme of the hymn is that each of us can make a choice to love others as God has loved us, and part of that message is that we can trust God in his power to forgive us, even if we feel we are inadequate and unworthy.

Frederick Faber, the writer of 'There's a Wideness in God's Mercy', had an unusual spiritual journey. He began life as a strict Calvinist, strongly opposed to the Roman Catholic Church, and went on to be ordained as an Anglican minister. In time, however, he came to feel that Anglican churches were too evangelical, and eventually chose to become a Catholic priest, for many years running the Brompton Oratory in London. He brought with him from the Protestant tradition his love of hymn singing, and he worked tirelessly writing hymns for Catholics to enjoy.

Frederick Faber's life of soul-searching for what he truly could believe required a deep trust in God's mercy and forgiveness as he made one life commitment, then changed his mind to make another. This hymn speaks emotively of what he felt was the overflowing nature of God's grace – and reminds us of our narrow view and limited understanding of the wealth of God's divine nature.

There's a wideness in God's mercy
like the wideness of the sea;
there's a kindness in his justice
which is more than liberty.

There is welcome for the sinner,
and more graces for the good;
there is mercy with the Saviour;
there is healing in his blood.

(Frederick William Faber, 1814–63)

To God Be the Glory

O perfect redemption, the purchase of blood!
To every believer the promise of God!
The vilest offender who truly believes,
that moment from Jesus a pardon receives.

(Fanny J. Crosby, 1820–1915)

In 1953, when Billy Graham and his Crusade team made their first visit to England, they brought with them one of the most popular of the thousands of gospel hymns written by the blind poetess, Fanny Crosby. 'To God Be the Glory' was an instant favourite, not least because of the confident statements of faith it contains. It praises God for his promise to pardon even the 'vilest offender', which leaves most of us feeling that however inadequate we might be at times, there is positive hope for us too!

Bind us together, Lord

Do you ever feel, especially when you watch the news or pick up a paper, that we are more interested in man's inhumanity to man than in how we might be able to make one another's lives easier, healthier, safer or fairer? And the most worrying thought is that the media are simply reflecting the world as it has become, a world in which hatred, distrust, greed and point-scoring mean more than tolerance and understanding.

It's as if we're heading back towards a tribal culture in which anyone who is different – in age, colour, background, language or ability – can become the object of derision, fear or complete indifference. It's shocking that our situation now has moved so far from the Christian vision of our world. What would Jesus' reaction be if he were to comment on the world around us today? Remembering his anger at the business deals and sharp practices going on in the Temple, and the way in which he actively sought out the company of those who were considered outcasts, we can imagine his fury and disbelief at the way in which nowadays money is king and power is everything. Whatever happened to 'loving thy neighbour'?

Every Christmas we pray for peace on earth. In fact, surely it is in our human nature to want to live alongside our neighbours in peace and prosperity? For centuries, that vision has been the plea of hymn writers, who have put their observations and longing into graphic, heartfelt verse that pricks the conscience and touches a chord in all caring people.

For me, that plea can be summed up in the song that Bob Gillman wrote in 1974. He was a printer by trade, but a writer of Country and Western-style songs for pleasure. He said that the words of 'Bind Us Together, Lord' 'popped into his head' while he was at a prayer meeting at a friend's house – and I think their simplicity, combined with the depth of longing he was plainly feeling, give his plea power and credence.

Bind us together, Lord,
bind us together
with cords that cannot be broken.
Bind us together, Lord,
bind us together,
O bind us together with love.

(Bob Gillman, b. 1946)

Almighty Father, who dost give
the gift of life to all who live,
look down on all earth's sin and strife,
and lift us to a nobler life.

Thy world is weary of its pain;
of selfish greed and fruitless gain;
of tarnished honour, falsely strong,
and all its ancient deeds of wrong.

(John Masterman, 1867–1933)

Back at the start of the twentieth century, John Masterman,
an Anglican priest who spent his latter years as a minister
in the naval towns of Portsmouth and Plymouth, summed

up his frustration that, having been given the wonderful gift of life, we've squandered the blessings of our surroundings in selfish pursuit. He prays that God might give us hope to lift us from the many wrongs that greed and ambition for personal gain have created in the world.

Timothy Dudley-Smith takes up the same theme in one verse of his much-loved modern classic, 'Lord, for the Years'. He recognizes the same world-weariness that John Masterman had seen years before, but adds the extra thought that it's our obsession with individual wealth and pleasure that blights our world and oppresses our spirit. Throughout his hymn, though, Timothy is confident of God's constancy. However lacking we are, God remains infinitely loving and caring.

Lord, for the Years

Lord, for our land, in this our generation,
    spirits oppressed by pleasure, wealth and care;
for young and old, for commonwealth and nation,
    Lord of our land, be pleased to hear our prayer.

(Timothy Dudley-Smith, b. 1926)

Christ is Alive, Let Christians Sing

In every insult, rift and war
where colour, scorn or wealth divide,
Christ suffers still, yet loves the more,
and lives, where even hope has died.

(Brian Wren, b. 1936)

Brian Wren was drawing upon considerable personal experience when he wrote this verse in his hymn 'Christ is
Alive'. Having been ordained a minister in the 1960s, he
soon got involved in a variety of practical ways in the hope
of making a difference to the poverty of body and soul he
saw in the world around him. He joined committees working for justice and peace and was an active organizing member of War on Want. He was appalled by the injustice that
left millions starving while others wasted so much of the
plenty available to them. As he points out in this verse, so
often it's the old divisions of wealth and skin colour that
lead to inhumanity and inequality around the world. And
yet, amid the hopelessness, Brian paints a vision of a loving
Christ who stands alongside those who suffer.

We've a story to tell to the nations,
that shall turn their hearts to the right,
a story of truth and mercy,
a story of peace and light.

We've a song to be sung to the nations,
that shall lift their hearts to the Lord,
a song that shall conquer evil
and shatter the spear and sword.

We've a Saviour to show to the nations,
who the path of sorrow hath trod,
that all of the world's great peoples
might come to the truth of God.

(H. Ernest Nichol, 1862–1928)

English musician and poet Ernest Nichol wrote this hymn in 1896 when the Victorian world was full of the missionary spirit as many brave and committed Christians left behind the world they knew to take the message of the gospel to far-flung lands. Those missionaries, and the quarter of a million or so others who have become missionaries since the end of the Second World War, understood all too well how prejudice and greed can bring despair and poverty to people who struggle simply to stay alive. Ernest Nichol believed that only by following Christ's loving example can we hope to find a solution to the world's troubles.

Modern-day writing team John Bell and Graham Maule of the Iona Community have come up with a song that echoes the hope felt by Ernest Nichol a century earlier. In Christ they see the perfect example of how we should live – without division caused by race, class, sex or language – working together in trust and common purpose to bring unity and understanding to all people, whoever and wherever they are.

Jesus Calls Us Here to Meet Him

Jesus calls us to each other;
found in him are no divides.
Race and class and sex and language;
such are barriers he derides.

Join the hands of friend and stranger;
join the hands of age and youth;
join the faithful and the doubter
in their common search for truth.

(John Bell and Graham Maule, b. 1949 and 1958)

91

Christ, from Whom All Blessings Flow

Many are we now, and one,
we who Jesus have put on;
there is neither bond nor free,
male nor female, Lord, in thee.

Love, like death, hath all destroyed,
rendered all distinctions void;
names and sects and parties fall;
thou, O Christ, art all in all!

(Charles Wesley, 1707–88)

Nearly three centuries ago, Charles Wesley and his preacher brother John forged the start of the Methodist Church by travelling more than 100,000 miles on foot and horseback in order to take the message of their faith to as many people around Britain as possible. They certainly weren't universally welcomed – quite the opposite, as there are countless stories of their being chased out of towns by angry gangs, attacked with sticks and having to hide beneath hedges until the coast was clear. They never lost their deep love for humanity, though. After each attack, they picked themselves up and carried on – which speaks not only of their courage and strength, but of the depth and certainty of their belief that God would protect them as long as they were doing his work. More than that, they showed a genuine love for everyone they met, whatever their background or circumstances. Charles expressed that love and their wish for fellowship among all people in these two hymns – 'Christ, from Whom All Blessings Flow' and 'Thou God of Truth and Life'.

Thou God of Truth and Life

Didst thou not make us one,
that we might one remain,
together travel on,
and bear each other's pain,
till all thy utmost goodness prove,
and rise renewed in perfect love?

Then let us ever bear
the blessed end in view,
and join, with mutual care,
to fight our passage through;
and kindly help each other on,
till all receive the starry crown.

(Charles Wesley, 1707–88)

Onward, Christian Soldiers

Like a mighty army
   moves the Church of God;
brothers, we are treading
   where the saints have trod:
we are not divided,
   all one body we,
one in hope and doctrine,
   one in charity.

(Sabine Baring-Gould, 1834–1924)

The Christian Church can be a powerful vehicle for God's love on earth. It doesn't matter about denomination. In fact, I remember being told very movingly by a young Sudanese man that in his country where Christians were a persecuted minority, just to meet a fellow Christian was cause for rejoicing! He had been terribly tortured for his faith – beaten to a pulp, fingernails torn out, electrodes put on his body, simply because he was a Christian who was outspoken on behalf of his faith and his basic rights. One hymn that spoke volumes to him was 'Onward, Christian Soldiers'. It's known around the world, even though it started life in 1864 in the small Yorkshire village of Horbury Bridge where the local curate, Sabine Baring-Gould, needed a hymn that local youngsters could march to as they processed through the village in traditional style on Whit Tuesday. During the previous evening, he 'knocked off' (to use his own words) a hymn which expresses confidence that God unifies us all in one faith and one church, and 'Onward, Christian Soldiers' has had us all marching ever since!

We are one in the Spirit, we are one in the Lord,
we are one in the Spirit, we are one in the Lord,
and we pray that all unity may one day be restored:
and they'll know we are Christians by our love, by our love,
yes, they'll know we are Christians by our love.

(Peter Scholtes, 1938–2009)

One of the defining features of Christians is their wish to show God's love by serving others. A typical example of this is the missionary spirit that has taken people to lands across the world where they have selflessly devoted their lives to the needs of others, often without recognition or reward. To commit ourselves to that extent would be impossible for most of us, but in any community you will find Christian people who spend their whole lives quietly helping out wherever they can. In fact, how often do you hear about someone who is a stalwart neighbour, always ready to lend a helping hand – only to learn later that your neighbour is also a Christian whose faith is very important? It's because of that that I love the sentiment of Peter Scholtes's hymn, with its line 'They'll Know We Are Christians by Our Love', because it expresses the belief that love in action will show people of other – or no – faith that we are Christians not just in name, but in deed as well.

That selflessness has been a feature of Christian work for centuries. Back in 1766, John Fawcett was just 26 years old when he brought his new bride, Mary, to begin their ministry at a poor Baptist church in Wainsgate. After seven years they were asked to take over a much larger and more influential church – but on the day they were due to leave, both they and their parishioners were so upset that they unloaded the wagons, and they stayed for the next 54 years in Wainsgate at the church where they felt they were needed most.

John became well known as a writer whose work was even noticed by King George III. The King promised John anything he wanted, but the offer was politely turned down. 'I have lived among my own people, enjoying their love,' wrote John. 'God has blessed my labours among them and I need nothing which even a King could supply.' John Fawcett understood the true value of fellowship and community, as we see in his hymn, 'Blest Be the Tie That Binds'.

Blest be the tie that binds
our hearts in Christian love;
the fellowship of kindred minds
 is like to that above.

We share our mutual woes,
our mutual burdens bear;
and often for each other flows
the sympathizing tear.

(John Fawcett, 1740–1817)

O brother man, fold to thy heart thy brother!
where pity dwells, the peace of God is there;
to worship rightly is to love each other,
each smile a hymn, each kindly deed a prayer.

(John Greenleaf Whittier, 1807–92)

It's odd that the wonderful American poet John Greenleaf
Whittier should even think of putting the word 'hymn' into
one of his verses because, as a Quaker, he was used to wor-
shipping in silence, certainly without music, and probably
without any real appreciation of how uplifting communal

hymn singing could be. However, the beauty and simplicity of his words have touched the souls of many down the years, and these inspirational words, matched with glorious music, make a thrilling combination.

'O Brother Man' is usually sung to the 'Londonderry Air', a melody that soars to a crescendo, taking all who sing it not just to a high note, but to a high level of involvement with the sentiment of the words. We are charged to 'fold to our hearts' our 'brother man' – *all*, regardless of background or faith. Unless we truly feel and show love to one another, then to proclaim ourselves worshippers of Christ is hollow. Christ showed love to everyone. So should we.

If there is one overriding theme that links together all the songs of talented writer and worship leader Dave Bilbrough, it's *love*. He gives thanks for the grace and faithfulness of God, but most of all he speaks of love – God's to us, and ours due to him. 'Let There Be Love Shared Among Us' has almost become an anthem of our time, a plea for God's presence as we reach out in love to all around us.

Let there be love shared among us,
let there be love in our eyes;
may now your love sweep this nation,
cause us, O Lord, to arise;
give us a fresh understanding

of brotherly love that is real,
let there be love shared among us,
let there be love.

(Dave Bilbrough, b. 1963)

Let there be peace on earth
and let it begin with me;
let there be peace on earth,
the peace that was meant to be.
With God as our Father,
brothers and sisters are we.
Let us walk with each other
in perfect harmony.

Let peace begin with me,
let this be the moment now;
with every step I take,
let this be my solemn vow;
to take each moment, and live each moment
in peace eternally.
Let there be peace on earth
and let it begin with me.

(Sy Miller and Jill Jackson)

Husband and wife team Sy Miller and Jill Jackson wrote this song so that one summer evening in 1955 a group of just under two hundred teenagers of all races, religions and backgrounds who were camping high in the California mountains could lock arms, form a circle and sing together this prayer for peace.

I'm sure I'm not alone in choosing this simple song, 'Let There Be Peace on Earth', as my absolute favourite of all hymns. It poses a straightforward challenge to us all – to take responsibility for the world in which we live. Why on earth should we think that the job of forging peace belongs to everyone else? Surely if we all play a loving part – making a positive difference in our own lives, families and communities – then from small beginnings a miracle could grow! Then perhaps that 'peace on earth' that the angels spoke of when they announced the coming of Christ will not simply be handed down from God – but will come through all of us using the gift of God's love to help build the world he meant this to be.

And to the weary, rest

Thy head upon my breast

Perhaps weariness is simply a fact of modern times. We all lead such frantic, problem-laden lives that the sheer challenge of coping and carrying on can leave the most optimistic of us worn down and worn out.

By weariness, what I definitely don't mean is tiredness. I think that too is an accepted part of our daily lives, but weariness is so much more than just the feeling that if you sit down for a moment you'll fall asleep for hours. That kind of fatigue is simply physical. Weariness plummets different depths within us. On the outside, we may appear fine. We carry on with our responsibilities with dogged determination, concealing the fact that both emotionally and spiritually we are exhausted, running on empty.

The trigger for such weariness is different for each of us,

but often it begins with circumstances way beyond our control. Marriage partners and family life can grind us down. The responsibility of being a parent can weigh heavy, as can the recognition that in time we become parents to our own mothers and fathers as they grow older. The loss of someone we love can tip us into grief and a sense of abandonment. The burden of our daily work and routine can become oppressive, perhaps bringing with it a sense of inadequacy at not being able to cope. A change in social standing, financial security or physical health may alter our perspective of ourselves and our worth to others. World politics may depress us, neighbours annoy us, friends seem distant. Doubts might creep in about what we really believe, so that we find ourselves asking whether there is actually a God who truly cares for each of us in a personal and life-changing way.

Such changes and experiences can lay us low, sapping our energy, limiting our resources and challenging our faith in ourselves and the world around us. And that kind of grinding worry *is* draining, bringing a total exhaustion that may give us blessed sleep to block out our thoughts for a while, but from which we wake feeling that our hours of slumber brought us no true rest at all.

I don't believe anyone is immune to such weariness at some time in life – and that's why it's an experience mentioned by hymn writers down the ages. They know the feeling. They recognize the challenges. They've faced those doubts. And in the passages that follow, you can see where they found understanding and comfort.

I heard the voice of Jesus say,
'Come unto me and rest;
lay down, thou weary one, lay down
thy head upon my breast.'

(Horatius Bonar, 1808–89)

Scottish minister Horatius Bonar looked to the Gospel of Matthew to find comfort for the weariness he not only sometimes felt himself, but sensed in others.

'Come to me, all you who are weary and burdened, and I will give you rest' (Matthew 11.28). Just this one verse, so simply written, has touched the hearts of many a weary, worn person over the years. There's no ambiguity here. God promises that if we come to him in whatever world-worn state we find ourselves, he will give us rest. It's not a promise to take away our burdens, because after that rest those problems will still be there. However, the rest we can find in God will help us discover the confidence, ability and strength we need to face the challenges of life with fresh purpose.

Jesus Shall Reign Where'er the Sun

Blessings abound where'er he reigns:
the prisoner leaps to lose his chains;
the weary find eternal rest,
and all the sons of want are blest.

(Isaac Watts, 1674–1748)

Over three centuries ago, Isaac Watts was someone to whom weariness was just a way of life. From an early age, he was dogged by ill health, which exhausted and frustrated him. He must have been quite unusual to look at – only five foot tall with a large head made even bigger by a huge wig, and small piercing eyes. This didn't endear him to the ladies. In fact, when he proposed to one lady love, she replied, 'I like the jewel but not the setting.' Can you imagine how that must have hurt?

But when worldly relationships proved trying, his relationship with God became all the more dear to him, and that deep belief was poured out in the hundreds of hymn texts he wrote. Like all hymn writers, his writing was informed by what was going on in his life – and it is very clear that his constant ill health sometimes wore him down. For him, though, the way to find that elusive and longed-for 'rest' was through Christ's blessing.

Courage, brother, do not stumble,
though thy path be dark as night;
there's a star to guide the humble;
trust in God, and do the right.
Let the road be rough and dreary,
and its end far out of sight,
foot it bravely, strong or weary,
trust in God, and do the right!

(Norman Macleod, 1812–72)

A hundred years or so later, nineteenth century Scottish minister Norman Macleod was based at the Barony Church in Glasgow where he saw first-hand the hardship, prejudice and unfairness faced by the working classes. He became their tireless champion, holding services to which only people in working clothes were admitted, setting up loan funds, savings banks, literacy schemes and housing initiatives. He campaigned to get buses and trams running and parks and museums open on Sundays so that they could be enjoyed by working people. He understood the weariness of the working man, and in this much-loved hymn he urges courage and trust in God as the way through dark times. His words touched the hearts of many, including Queen Victoria herself, who sought his company as a confidant after she heard a sermon he gave in Crathie Church in 1854.

Sing of the Lord's Goodness

Courage in our darkness, comfort in our sorrow,
Spirit of our God most high;
solace for the weary, pardon for the sinner,
splendour of the living God.

Come, then, all you nations,
sing of your Lord's goodness,
melodies of praise and thanks to God.
Ring out the Lord's glory,
praise him with your music,
worship him and bless his name!

(Ernest Sands, b. 1949)

Sometimes it's hard to find the energy or courage to work through the problems that weary us and keep us awake at night – but in 1981 Ernest Sands wrote an upbeat hymn about what he considers we need most when worries become a burden – to recognize and be thankful for all the good things with which we are blessed.

How sweet the name of Jesus sounds
in a believer's ear!
It soothes his sorrows, heals his wounds,
and drives away his fear.

It makes the wounded spirit whole,
and calms the troubled breast;
'tis manna to the hungry soul,
and to the weary, rest.

(John Newton, 1725–1807)

These great words come from John Newton, a man who saw the dregs of the world and was eventually worn down by what he saw. He'd been dragged into the navy as a teenager, flogged for desertion, travelled the world as a slave trader, and finally nearly drowned in a dreadful storm at sea before going through a miraculous conversion experience that changed his life from world-weary to God-centred. The words of his hymns always hit right at the heart of our experience, and I'm sure that's because he'd seen so much that burdened his conscience and oppressed him. And don't you think that the words 'wounded spirit' describe exactly how it feels to be wearied by life?

Lead Us, Heavenly Father, Lead Us

Saviour, breathe forgiveness o'er us:
    all our weakness thou dost know;
thou didst tread this earth before us,
    thou didst feel its keenest woe;
lone and dreary, faint and weary,
    through the desert thou didst go.

(James Edmeston, 1791–1867)

In early Victorian times, James Edmeston lived in Stepney in the East End of London where there was so much hardship and poverty that sadness and despair were a way of life. Through it all, he believed in hope and commitment – and because he wanted to do all he could to alleviate the suffering he saw around him, he became very involved with the children of the London Orphan Asylum. There he met children who had never known love or comfort in the whole of their young lives, children who were born weary. For them he wrote a new hymn every Sunday, and in one of his best known and loved hymns, he reassures his young congregation that however worn-down and unloved they might feel, Jesus understood all too well because he'd felt just the same during his time on earth.

He Lives

In all the world around me, I see his loving care,
and though my heart grows weary, I never will despair;
I know that he is leading through all the stormy blast;
the day of his appearing will come at last.

He lives, he lives, salvation to impart!
You ask me how I know he lives?
He lives within my heart.

(Alfred H. Ackley, 1887–1960)

When you're in the grip of deep weariness, you can feel
dreadfully alone – and however much those who love you
try to understand, and may even identify with the way you
feel from parallels in their own lives, the experience is yours
alone. In that lonely place, how comforting it is to believe
that you are not alone on the journey and that your footsteps are being guided towards rest and well-being. That
was the thought captured by Alfred Ackley when he wrote
these words in the 1930s. He understood the reassurance
that comes from believing that God's presence and love can
help us through the darkest times in our lives.

109

Safe in the Arms of Jesus,
Safe from corroding care,
Safe from the world's temptations,
Sin cannot harm me there.
Free from the blight of sorrow,
Free from my doubts and fears;
  Only a few more trials,
  Only a few more tears.

Safe in the arms of Jesus,
Safe on his gentle breast,
There by his love o'ershaded,
Sweetly my soul shall rest.

(Fanny Crosby, 1820–1915)

You'd expect someone who lives to the age of 95 to be admirably fit and healthy, yet Fanny Crosby faced the lifelong challenge of blindness, which meant that every action, movement and decision required careful planning – and probably the help of others. That would be wearying enough in itself, but imagine how exhausting it must have been for her to write so many thousands of hymn texts in her lifetime that sometimes she was turning out two or three a day! 'Safe in the Arms of Jesus' is one of her most loved because, although her words speak eloquently of the sorrow, doubt, care and fear which seem to be an inevitable part of the human condition, there is such reassurance and comfort in the image she creates of Christ welcoming us into the safety and peace of his embrace.

In God alone my soul will find rest and peace,
in God my peace and joy.
Only in God my soul shall find its rest,
find its rest and peace.

(Taizé chant, based on Psalm 62)

Have you ever had the chance to visit Taizé, the monastic community in France, which welcomes thousands of mainly young Christians to join in their worship each day? The chants of Taizé are now used in church services around the world. What I like most about them is the way they get right to the heart of how we feel. They are universal prayers relating to common human reactions, which is why they touch us where we really are, putting into simple words our longing for comfort, reassurance and a real connection with God.

For the Taizé chant 'In God Alone', a simple, melodious tune has been chosen to accompany words that echo

Psalm 62. Writing three thousand years ago, the psalmist was experiencing that same longing for peace and rest that's all too familiar to us today. The words might be ancient, but can you think of a better way to word your hope for relief from world-weariness?

Softly and tenderly Jesus is calling,
calling for you and for me;
see, on the portals he's waiting and watching,
watching for you and for me.

Come home, come home,
ye who are weary, come home!
Earnestly, tenderly Jesus is calling,
calling, O sinner, come home!

(William L. Thompson, 1847–1909)

'Softly and Tenderly' is a special favourite of mine because of the moving story I heard from Jeannie, a lovely lady who was both the daughter and wife of Peterhead fishermen right up in the north of Scotland. Some years ago, her father and husband went down on the same fishing boat, and grief and loss are still etched in her face, along with the weariness that comes from coping alone with a young family to raise. She said she's always been comforted by the thought of Jesus calling with gentleness and welcome to the men she loved as they lost their lives and went to join him – and it's this hymn that creates that reassuring picture for her.

Others, too, have caught that note of comforting reassurance. The American civil rights leader Martin Luther King loved this hymn so much that it was sung at his memorial service in Ebenezer Baptist Church, Atlanta, Georgia on 8 April 1968.

Count your blessings

Do you ever feel there just aren't enough hours in the day to get everything done that you mean to accomplish? I sometimes wish I could have a couple of hours each day that no one else knows about – time to catch up, draw breath, time just to be *me*! Life today is so busy and stressful that it has us falling exhausted into bed at the end of each day, only to toss and turn with worry at times during the night. However different from one another we may seem to be, I think, because we're all simply human, the same sort of worries concern us all, even if the actual circumstances differ. We fret about family, relationships, illness, loss, grief, making our money stretch, finding the right job, loneliness, grey hairs, thickening waistlines, fitness, security and our longing for love.

And as if our own personal problems aren't enough, we have the world to worry about! Will our children grow up in a world of peace? Will pollution and global warming destroy the planet? Will we die from the next flu pandemic, or from chemical fertilizers, nuclear bombs or biological warfare? Our television screens are filled with terrifying blockbusters about the knife edge on which our civilization is balanced – and the facts on our news bulletins don't seem all that far removed from the fiction of Hollywood. Life is complex. Communities are breaking down; neighbours are unknown to us; crime is rising – and so is our fear for ourselves, our families and their future.

Yes, this is a lot to worry about – but we have to keep things in perspective. Most of us have plenty of food on the table, comfortable homes to live in, family or friends who may niggle us at times but who would be right beside us if we were in trouble. If we're ill, we have doctors and hospitals to treat us. If we're out of work or retired, there's money available to help us through. If we need entertainment, we have books, theatre, films, television, computers, music and mobile phones. We can take part in sports, dance, paint, tend our gardens, visit friends, nip out for a drink or a meal, have barbecues, go to the seaside, keep pets, sail, swim, fish, fly, walk, shout, laugh and jump for joy!

Do you remember the old conundrum about looking at a glass that is half-filled with water? How would you describe it? Would you say it was half *full* or half *empty*? And if that glass represented your own life, how would you describe it then? Well, my glass is more than half full! It's overflowing! Of course, there are the usual worries and grumbles, but they are far outweighed by the many blessings around me – people I love, things I cherish, talents I value, surroundings that are dear to me, and an overwhelming sense of optimism and contentment. I'm glad to be alive! I'm grateful for every second of every day! 'Count your blessings', says the hymn – and I do – but God knows I lose count because there are too many to number.

Count Your Blessings

When you look at others with their lands and gold,
think that Christ has promised you his wealth untold;
count your many blessings, money cannot buy
your reward in heaven nor your home on high!

Count your blessings, name them one by one;
count your many blessings, see what God hath done!

(Johnson Oatman, Jr, 1856–1922)

New every morning is the love
our wakening and uprising prove;
through sleep and darkness safely brought,
restored to life and power and thought.

Old friends, old scenes will lovelier be
as more of heaven in each we see:
some softening gleam of love and prayer
shall dawn on every cross and care.

(John Keble, 1792–1866)

Do you ever wake up with that 'Glad that I live am I!' feeling? I often do, because for me it's at the start of the day, when my eyes are getting accustomed to the light creeping round the curtains, that I spend a few precious minutes thinking about and planning the day ahead. I'm definitely an early bird – and the flip side of that is that I'm generally good for nothing after about ten o'clock at night!

John Keble spent his last 30 years as the vicar in the small village of Hursley in Hampshire, but his earlier career had been one of academic excellence. His skill as a word-smith was recognized when he became Professor of Poetry at Oxford University, and his lyrical, descriptive words led to many of his poems being combined with music to become hymns. On a note attached to the words of this hymn, he quoted from Lamentations 3.21–22, 'His compassions fail not. They are new every morning.' So this hymn is an outpouring of thanks that he had once again been brought through the night ready to face the day ahead. More than that, he seems to feel that his daily, prayerful rededication of what he sees as the many blessings in his life makes even the most familiar sights, relationships and experiences feel like a little bit of heaven.

I Sing the Mighty Power of God

I sing the goodness of the Lord, that filled the earth
    with food;
he formed the creatures with his word and then
    pronounced them good.
Lord, how thy wonders are displayed where'er I turn
    my eye:
if I survey the ground I tread or gaze upon the sky!

I sing the wisdom that ordained the sun to rule the day,
the moon shines full at his command, and all the
    stars obey.

(Isaac Watts, 1674–1748)

Of the seven hundred or so hymns composed by Isaac Watts, some, like this one, were written specifically with children in mind. 'I Sing the Mighty Power of God' first appeared in a book called *Divine Songs for Children* – and I wonder if he was thinking of children singing during what we now call 'school assemblies' when he thanked God for ordering the sun to start the day, and the moon to shine at night?

This next hymn, full of wonder at the beauty around us, is one of the most popular hymns sung widely today. Its writer, Folliott Sandford Pierpoint, lived in and around Bath in the west country. I remember one *Songs of Praise* programme when I stood, as Folliott did, on the hill looking out over the Wye Valley, which inspired him to write these graphic words. And I remember thinking it would be hard to gaze over that view and not be moved to wonder and gratitude for God's gifts to us on earth.

> **For the beauty of the earth,**
> for the beauty of the skies,
> for the love which from our birth
> over and around us lies.
>
> For each perfect gift of thine,
> to our race so freely given,
> graces human and divine,
> flowers of earth and buds of heaven:

Christ our God, to thee we raise
this our sacrifice of praise!

(Folliott Sandford Pierpoint, 1835–1917)

O Lord my God, when I in awesome wonder
consider all the works thy hand hath made,
I see the stars, I hear the mighty thunder,
thy power throughout the universe displayed.

Then sings my soul, my Saviour God, to thee,
how great thou art, how great thou art!
Then sings my soul, my Saviour God to thee,
how great thou art, how great thou art!

(Carl Boberg, 1859–1940, trans. Stuart K. Hine, 1899–1989)

When it comes to giving thanks for all God's wonderful gifts, this old favourite takes the biscuit! During the twenty and more years that I've been presenting *Songs of Praise*, 'How Great Thou Art' has consistently been chosen by our viewers as their most popular hymn. The words weren't written in English at all, but were translated by missionary Stuart Hine, who heard it sung in the Ukraine nearly forty years after it had originally been written in Swedish by Carl Boberg, an evangelical journalist.

Carl had returned to his home town of Monsteras on the south-east coast of Sweden as a preacher, and it was there, in 1886, that these words came to him as he looked across the waters of the Monsteras inlet to see a rainbow forming after a violent storm. The beauty of the scene following the terrifying power of the thunder and lightning formed in his mind these words of wonder, joy, reassurance and 'humble adoration' that have inspired others to praise ever since.

This next hymn, also by a Swede, was written in 1891, only four years after Carl Boberg wrote 'How Great Thou Art'. August Storm became a Christian at a Salvation Army meeting in Stockholm, and went on to become one of the Army's leading officers. When he wrote the words of 'Thanks to God' for the Swedish equivalent of *The War Cry* newspaper, he began every line with the word 'thanks' – 32 in all! It may well have been his experience of working with vulnerable and needy people that made him realize that it's not just the good things in life for which we need to give thanks. Character is never formed through easy living, and it is when times are hard that we really discover what our strengths and weaknesses are. For that reason, Storm gives thanks for pain and pleasure, poverty and wealth, clouds and sunshine, knowing that by working our way through all that life throws our way, we become what God truly intends us to be.

Thanks to God

Thanks for thorns as well as roses,
thanks for weakness and for health,
thanks for clouds as well as sunshine,
thanks for poverty and wealth!
Thanks for pain as well as pleasure,
all thou sendest day by day;
and thy Word, our dearest treasure,
  shedding light upon our way.

Thanks for daily toil and labour
and for rest when shadows fall;
thanks for love of friend and neighbour,
and thy goodness unto all!

(August Ludvig Storm, 1862–1914,
trans. Carl E. Backstrom, 1901)

We Plough the Fields, and Scatter

We thank thee then, O Father,
  for all things bright and good;
the seed-time and the harvest,
  our life, our health, our food.

No gifts have we to offer
   for all thy love imparts,
but that which thou desirest,
   our humble, thankful hearts:

All good gifts around us
   are sent from heaven above;
then thank the Lord, O thank the Lord
   for all his love.

(Matthias Claudius, 1740–1815,
trans. Jane Montgomery Campbell, 1817–78)

Harvest just wouldn't be the same without the chance to sing together, 'We Plough the Fields, and Scatter'. This hymn is so associated with the traditional festivals held by every church in autumn to give thanks to God for the bounty of the harvest, which keeps us fed for yet another year. Nowadays supermarkets with their packaged and frozen foods detach us from the land and its gifts to us, so it's important and heartwarming each year to recognize that, however sophisticated farming has become, at the heart of all we eat and enjoy is God's creation. This hymn, originally written by Matthias Claudius, a newspaper journalist in Germany, and partnered with the melody from an old peasants' song, was translated into English by a vicar's daughter, Jane Montgomery Campbell, for a hymn book she was compiling for children.

The Wonder of It All

There's the wonder of sunset at evening,
    the wonder as sunrise I see;
but the wonder of wonders that thrills my soul
is the wonder that God loves me.

O, the wonder of it all! The wonder of it all!
Just to think that God loves me.

(George Beverly Shea, b. 1909)

George Beverly Shea took up the theme of the blessing and contentment to be found in God's love in his song 'The Wonder of It All'. He always said that he was prompted to write these words while on his way to a Billy Graham rally in Scotland. On board the *SS United States*, bound for Southampton, he'd got into conversation with another passenger, who wanted to know what the rallies were like. George tried to describe the response that usually followed Dr Graham's invitation to the audience to come to the stage if they wanted to become Christians, and he found himself saying that 'watching people by the hundreds come forward . . . oh, the wonder of it all!' That phrase stayed with him, and later that night he wrote both the words and the melody of this simple song, which captures his awe of a God who is powerful enough to create the beauty and complexity of the world around us yet who still 'loves me' in a really personal way.

One of my favourite hymns thanking God for his many blessings is 'Now Thank We All Our God', which I love because it helped me to find a title for both my first novel, *With Hearts and Hymns and Voices*, and my Premier Christian Radio series, *Hearts and Hymns*. You'll notice that I've altered one very important word, changing 'hands' to 'hymns', because it seemed to me that to talk about my many years of experience on *Songs of Praise* could well be described as a wonderful story in which 'hearts' and 'hymns' have an equal role!

What is most amazing about this hymn is the fact that it was written at a time of tremendous hardship and yet rings with praise and gratitude! Martin Rinkart, the son of a coppersmith, returned as a pastor to his own village of Eilenburg for the last half of his life. It was a time of rival pillaging armies, as well as plague. In the end, the toll of villagers who Rinkart himself buried was 4,000, sometimes in mass funerals for as many as 50 at a time.

On top of all that, after the plague came severe famine. When the Swedish forces occupying Eilenburg demanded a tax of 30,000 thalers from the despairing villagers, Rinkart appealed to them for mercy until the sum was finally reduced to 2,000 thalers. Perhaps he wrote this great hymn of thanks and praise on the evening he achieved that – no one is quite sure. What is certain is that this hymn, which lists so many of the blessings most of us enjoy in life, is nothing less than inspirational when sung to the accompaniment of a booming and glorious organ!

Now thank we all our God
with heart and hands and voices,
  who wondrous things hath done,
in whom his world rejoices;
    who from our mothers' arms
    hath blessed us on our way
    with countless gifts of love,
    and still is ours today.

(Martin Rinkart, 1586–1649,
trans. Catherine Winkworth, 1829–78)

Let us, with a gladsome mind,
praise the Lord, for he is kind:
  For his mercies ay endure,
  ever faithful, ever sure.

(John Milton, 1608–74, based on Psalm 136)

John Milton certainly was blessed with extraordinary talents, for which he constantly thanked God. He was only 15 years old when he wrote this paraphrase of Psalm 136, and as his skill and reputation as a poet, pamphleteer and writer grew, he eventually came to be regarded as second only to Shakespeare in the roll call of great English poets. He was outspoken and controversial in many of his views, in his defence of the freedom of speech and of the press, for instance, as well as in his canvassing in favour of divorce. Milton's outspoken dissatisfaction with humankind led to his being arrested and fined for his views in 1660 – but even though he was afflicted with total blindness in his early forties, he carried on expressing his gratefulness to God in his writing, especially in his masterpiece, *Paradise Lost*, which he finished in 1665.

O Praise Ye the Lord!

O praise ye the Lord! Thanksgiving and song
to him be outpoured all ages along:
for love in creation, for heaven restored,
for grace of salvation, O praise ye the Lord!

(Henry Williams Baker, 1821–77)

It's not often that a humble country vicar on the English–Welsh border is legitimately able to call himself 'Sir' but Sir Henry Williams Baker could do just that when he inherited his father's baronetcy shortly after arriving at Monkland, near Leominster. Henry loved hymns, writing a few himself, but mostly encouraging others to write, as well as unearthing translations of ancient Latin hymns that he didn't want to be lost to the Church. 'O Praise Ye the Lord', based on Psalms 148 and 150, is a magnificent anthem of praise, which is used universally in churches today. This one verse sums up the heart of our faith, our relationship with God and the manifold examples of God's goodness to us.

Tell out, my soul, the greatness of the Lord!
    Unnumbered blessings, give my spirit voice;
tender to me the promise of his word;
    in God my Saviour shall my heart rejoice.

(Timothy Dudley-Smith, b. 1926)

Timothy Dudley-Smith's modern paraphrase of the Magnificat recalls Mary's gratitude and trust when she first heard that she'd been chosen to become the mother of the Son of God. In spite of her central role in the story of Christ on earth, her recognition of God's blessings in her life is not so different from ours today. She feels joyful and secure in the knowledge of 'the promise of his word' – and as we consider the 'unnumbered blessings' in our own lives, we too can trust God with grateful joy.

When I Survey the Wondrous Cross

Were the whole realm of nature mine,
   that were a present far too small;
love so amazing, so divine,
   demands my soul, my life, my all.

(Isaac Watts, 1674–1748)

This one verse in Isaac Watts' magnificent hymn 'When I Survey' is one of my absolute favourites. So much is contained in four short lines – the enormous, awe-inspiring fact of God's love creating everything around us and all we need.

Isaac Watts' response to this huge thought is that if God has shown that much love to us, then the very least he can give in response is 'my soul, my life, my all'! I defy anyone to sing these words to that familiar melody 'Rockingham' without feeling a sense of commitment to, and security because of, our faith in a loving God.

Protect us wheresoe'er we go

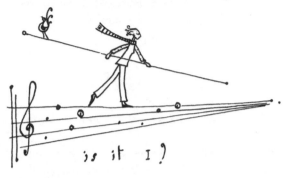

We think of God in many different roles. Sometimes he is an omnipotent, all-powerful King, too high above for us to think of him with anything other than awe and fear. At others, he is as close to us as the dearest of our friends, a companion in our loneliness, compassionate in our sadness and in complete empathy with all our muddled thoughts and emotions. In that respect, the role he fills in our lives is not unlike that of a parent – sometimes forbidding and judgemental, but mostly unconditionally loving and caring. There's something about the range of attitudes we are used to seeing in our own parents that is reassuringly protective, as if, childlike, we are only allowed to stray so far before we are rescued, guided back and comforted.

I'm sure many of our most familiar hymn texts were

originally an expression of prayer, as the writers put into words their plea to be watched over, restrained, guided and comforted by the God they think and speak of as their 'Father' The hymn, above all, that captures that for me is Henry Francis Lyte's great anthem in which he starts by praising the omnipotent 'King of heaven', but goes on to describe how, like a father, God knows us intimately, accepting our weaknesses and loving us all the same. I especially like the line, 'In his hands he gently bears us' – almost like an injured animal being nursed back to health in body, mind and spirit. When we are secure in the knowledge that we are cared for and protected, the trials of life can seem less threatening and alarming.

Praise, My Soul, the King of Heaven

Father-like, he tends and spares us,
  well our feeble frame he knows;
in his hands he gently bears us,
  rescues us from all our foes:
Praise him! Praise him!
Praise him! Praise him!
Widely as his mercy flows.

(Henry Francis Lyte, 1793–1847)

> **Jesu, lover of my soul,**
> let me to thy bosom fly,
> while the nearer waters roll,
> while the tempest still is high.
> Hide me, O my Saviour, hide,
> till the storm of life is past;
> safe into the haven guide;
> O receive my soul at last.

(Charles Wesley, 1707–88)

In this hymn, Charles Wesley pictures our lives as ships ploughing through smooth waters and raging seas – and somehow that image feels quite appropriate, even for those of us who are definitely landlubbers! We often do feel thrown around by the storms of life – sailing through peacefully most of the time, but every now and then knocked off our feet by insecurity, arguments, disappointment, betrayal, failure and exhaustion. It's at times like those that, even though we're grown adults, we may simply not know what to do for the best. Our instinct may be to curl up and hope our problems will go away – or, at the very least, hope that help, comfort and protection might be there for us just when we need it most.

The Christian belief, expressed so eloquently by Charles Wesley, is that help is *always* there, and that even though we may only become aware of God's love and protection through the very human presence of those around us, it is ultimately God who is cupping us in his caring hand.

Eternal Father, Strong to Save

O Trinity of love and power,
our brethren shield in danger's hour;
from rock and tempest, fire and foe,
protect them wheresoe'er they go:
    and ever let there rise to thee
    glad hymns of praise from land and sea.

(William Whiting, 1825–78)

I can't think of the image of our lives as a ship facing both calm and stormy waters without mentioning one of my all-time favourite hymns, 'Eternal Father, Strong to Save'. I grew up in a naval family, so this hymn always had special significance at school assemblies, when so many of us had fathers who were away at sea for weeks and sometimes months at a time. Even though this hymn is likely to be sung at almost every naval service because it asks so emotively for God's protection for vulnerable seamen and their vessels, it's likely that William Whiting never imagined his hymn being used in this way. He was a master of the quiristers (the local name for choristers) at Winchester Cathedral College, which is a long way inland from the sea! It's said he wrote these words for a young quirister who was about to set sail for America – and in doing so he created a powerful prayer that applies not only to our seamen, but to all of us longing for God's protection as we navigate the challenging journey of our lives.

The official hymn of the Boys' Brigade, 'Will Your Anchor Hold', by Victorian writer Priscilla Owens, once again pictures our lives as ships at sea. Its rousing chorus, in which our hope in God is likened to a solid anchor which keeps us – mind, body and soul – in safety, is great to sing at the top of your voice when you need a reminder of God's loving protection!

Will Your Anchor Hold in the Storms of Life?

We have an anchor that keeps the soul
steadfast and sure while the billows roll;
fastened to the Rock which cannot move,
grounded firm and deep in the Saviour's love!

(Priscilla Owens, 1829–99)

For All the Saints

Thou wast their rock, their fortress, and their might;
  thou, Lord, their Captain in the well-fought fight;
  thou, in the darkness drear, their one true Light.
  Alleluia!

(William Walsham How, 1823–97)

Two hymns that praise God as an all-powerful protector. In 'For All the Saints', William Walsham How conjures up an image of God protecting the faithful in battle, though this Victorian bishop, who spent his life as such a champion of the working man, had no practical experience of 'battle' at all. However, in his work among the poor of east London and the factory and mill workers of West Yorkshire, he would have been aware that for many of his congregation, life was a constant battle against poverty, illness and hopelessness. His picture of God's care as a rock and a fortress must have been very encouraging for them, as it is for us.

When Sir Robert Grant wrote 'O Worship the King', he went back to the imagery the writer of Psalm 104 had in mind of God's chariot formed from deep thunder-clouds, conjuring up a picture of an all-powerful God able to shield and defend his people from all harm. Sir Robert goes on to recognize that because our lives are short and our humanity makes us feeble and frail, above all we need to trust in God

135

as a powerful protector as well as our friend, with intimate knowledge of each and every one of us expressed in his personal care for us all.

O worship the King, all-glorious above;
O gratefully sing his power and his love;
   our shield and defender, the Ancient of Days,
   pavilioned in splendour and girded with praise.

Frail children of dust, and feeble as frail,
in thee do we trust, nor find thee to fail;
   thy mercies how tender, how firm to the end,
   Our Maker, Defender, Redeemer and Friend.

(Sir Robert Grant, 1779–1838)

Hail to the Lord's Anointed

He comes with succour speedy
   to those who suffer wrong;
to help the poor and needy,
   and bid the weak be strong;

> to give them songs for sighing,
> their darkness turn to light,
> whose souls, condemned and dying
> were precious in his sight.

(James Montgomery, 1771–1854)

James Montgomery was a man who understood the feeling of being needy, condemned and in darkness because on two occasions he was thrown into prison for his beliefs. He was a journalist, who when he was only 23 took over a Sheffield newspaper known for its extreme political views. Through it, he championed the cause of teaching children in Sunday school to write, which many in authority felt would instil dangerous ideas into working-class youth! He was also strongly opposed to slavery and the use of climbing-boys by chimney sweeps. His outspoken views, which were always based on his passionately held Christian principles, often landed him in trouble with the authorities – so his need to feel God's protection and his longing to be 'precious in his sight' must have been very real in the face of such physical opposition and hardship.

Come, Holy Ghost, Our Souls Inspire

Anoint and cheer our soiled face
with the abundance of thy grace:
keep far our foes, give peace at home;
where thou art guide no ill can come.

(*Veni Creator Spiritus*, ninth century,
trans. John Cosin, 1594–1672)

These words from a Latin hymn have been in continual use since the ninth century, which makes this seventeenth-century translation by John Cosin a relative youngster! The words are taken from a plainsong prayer that was sung at Whitsun, accompanied by the ringing of bells, the lighting of candles and the aroma of incense. By the eleventh century it was being used regularly in services to ordinate priests and consecrate bishops, and that practice continues today. Surely, as priests take vows to dedicate their lives to God's service, this prayer for God's protection and peace is particularly appropriate, especially when it's combined with an acknowledgement of their unworthiness and sin expressed in the description of 'our soiled face'. We often feel that because of mistakes we've made in our lives, we are unworthy of God's love. After all, if we're not prepared to follow him faithfully, why should he bother with us? This prayer recognizes our need for God's guidance, and our hope that in spite of everything we are *not* – as well as everything we *are* – he will still care for us.

Reassurance that God hears our regret and prayers when we know we've not come up to scratch is the theme of Daniel Schutte's popular modern hymn, 'I, the Lord'. This modern classic has become a worldwide favourite, mostly, I think, because he's created a poignant dialogue between God himself and all of us who find it too easy to ignore his call. Each plaintive verse puts into words some of the provoking, even upsetting, questions with which God constantly challenges us – questions we often choose to ignore. But respond we do, in every chorus!

> **I, the Lord of sea and sky,**
> I have heard my people cry.
> All who dwell in dark and sin
> my hand will save.
>
> *Here I am, Lord. Is it I, Lord?*
> *I have heard you calling in the night.*
> *I will go, Lord, if you lead me.*
> *I will hold your people in my heart.*

(Daniel Schutte, b. 1947)

Trusting Jesus

Singing, if my way is clear,
praying, if the path be drear;
if in danger, for him call,
trusting Jesus – that is all.

(Edgar Page Stites, 1836–1921)

Edgar Stites had to learn to trust Jesus in times of great danger and hardship while he was serving in the American Civil War, as well as later when he became a riverboat pilot. Like Sir Henry Baker in the next hymn, the famous paraphrase of Psalm 23, Edgar expresses his belief that simple trust is what is required of us all – that in spite of how we feel about ourselves, or however much we may fail in our attempts to live according to Christian principles, God will respond to our plea for protection and comfort providing we simply trust that he will do so.

The King of love my shepherd is,
whose goodness faileth never;
I nothing lack if I am his
and he is mine for ever.

(Henry Williams Baker, 1821–77)

What a Friend We Have in Jesus

Are we weak and heavy-laden,
cumbered with a load of care?
Jesus only is our refuge:
take it to the Lord in prayer.
Do thy friends despise, forsake thee?
Take it to the Lord in prayer;
in his arms he'll take and shield thee;
thou wilt find a solace there.

(Joseph Scriven, 1820–86)

When we think of our true friends, we can see that our relationships are mostly based on liking, knowledge and acceptance, and abiding trust that we can rely on one another to be there when needed. It's not surprising, then, that many hymn writers hoping for comfort and guidance in everyday life speak of their longing to have Christ as their 'friend'. Friends know all about us, the good, the bad and the ugly, and they love us in spite of it all! That's the understanding and acceptance we long for from God.

Joseph Scriven grew up in a wealthy family in Ireland, and it was there that, on the night before his wedding, his fiancée drowned. That tragedy upset him so much that he decided to leave his comfortable home to build a life on the other side of the world, in Canada, where his devotion to others in need earned him the title 'the Good Samaritan of Port Hope'. Apart from his own experience of sorrow, he saw such suffering during his life's work that he wrote his famous hymn, 'What a Friend We Have in Jesus', in which he shared his belief that he could only find the solace and support he needed in his dearest friend, Jesus.

It was the suffering of a bedridden friend that prompted Civilla Martin to write the charming hymn, 'His Eye is on the Sparrow'. When Civilla asked her friend if she ever got discouraged because of her illness, the reply was that if God cared for each little sparrow, he certainly cared for her! Mrs Martin translated those words of simple trust into a hymn that ever since has brought reassurance to many in need of God's father-like protection and friendship.

His Eye is on the Sparrow

Why should I feel discouraged, why should the
    shadows come,
why should my heart be lonely and long for
    Heav'n and home,
when Jesus is my portion? My constant Friend is he;
his eye is on the sparrow, and I know he watches me.

(Civilla Martin, 1869–1948)

Leaning on the Everlasting Arms

What have I to dread, what have I to fear,
leaning on the everlasting arms?
I have blessed peace with my Lord so near,
leaning on the everlasting arms.

(Elisha A. Hoffman, 1839–1929)

In the months leading up to 1887, when this much-loved
hymn was first published, successful author, businessman
and devout Presbyterian Anthony Showalter received two
sad letters from friends telling him of recent bereavements.
Searching for words to comfort them, he found Deuteron-
omy 33.27: 'The eternal God is your refuge, and underneath are the everlasting arms.' These words touched him
so much that he thought they would make an inspirational
hymn text – except he couldn't write poetry! That decided
him to ask his friend Elisha Hoffman, a pastor and author
of more than two thousand gospel songs, to help him weave
the thought into a hymn. Together they produced 'Leaning
on the Everlasting Arms' with its assurance of God's constant care, protection and fellowship.

That same sense of God's all-encompassing protection
'over me, underneath me, all around me' is the theme of a
prayerful hymn, 'O the Deep, Deep Love of Jesus', written
by the well-known Plymouth Brethren evangelist, Samuel

Trevor Francis, which was first published in London in 1898. This verse captures the nature of God's love, rolling towards us as relentlessly as the ocean, never stopping or turning in spite of everything we do to disappoint him. We are all so aware of our own failings that sometimes it's easy to feel that God would never be bothered with *us* – except he is, and his loving protection of us is like a mantle of care around our shoulders.

O the deep, deep love of Jesus,
vast, unmeasured, boundless, free!
rolling as a mighty ocean
in its fullness over me!
Underneath me, all around me,
is the current of thy love
leading onward, leading homeward,
to my glorious rest above.

(Samuel Trevor Francis, 1834–1925)

God be with you till we meet again;
'neath his wings protecting hide you;
daily manna still provide you;
God be with you till we meet again.

Till we meet, till we meet,
Till we meet at Jesus' feet,
Till we meet, till we meet,
God be with you till we meet again.

(Jeremiah Eames Rankin, 1828–1904)

This is one of my all-time favourite hymns because it's a blessing on those we love as we part company from them. This hymn isn't a prayer for our own protection, but for theirs, with words that are simple and sincere. Dr Jeremiah Rankin, the black American preacher, who wrote these words in the 1890s, loved congregational singing. Countless church services have ended with this benediction ever since - and can you think of a better way to ask for God's care to protect those we love than these timeless words? I wish the same to you now – that God's arms will be protecting and providing for you all the days of your life.

Acknowledgements

Every effort has been made to seek permission to use copyright material reproduced in this book. The publisher apologizes for those cases where permission might not have been sought and, if notified, will formally seek permission at the earliest opportunity.

The publisher and author acknowledge with thanks permission to reproduce extracts from the following:

A Touching Place, from John L. Bell and Graham Maule, *Love From Below* (Wild Goose Publications, 1989). Words and music: John L. Bell and Graham Maule. Copyright © 1989 WGRG, Iona Community, Glasgow G2 3DH, Scotland, wgrg@iona.org.uk; www.wgrg.co.uk.

As the Deer Pants by Martin Nystrom, copyright © 1983 Restoration Music Ltd/Sovereign Music UK, P.O. Box 356, Leighton Buzzard LU7 3WP, UK. Reproduced by permission.

Because He Lives by William J. Gaither and Gloria Gaither, copyright © 1971 Gaither Music Company/kingswaysongs.com.*
*Published by kingswaysongs.com for the UK and Eire; tym@kingsway.co.uk. Used by permission.

Benediction (May God's Blessing Surround You), copyright © Cliff Barrows. Used with permission.

Bind Us Together, Lord by Bob Gillman, copyright © 1977 Thankyou Music.*
*Adm. by worshiptogether.com songs, excl. UK and Europe, adm. by kingswaysongs.com; tym@kingsway.co.uk. Used by permission.

147

Acknowledgements

Brother, Sister, Let Me Serve You (The Servant Song) by Richard Gillard, © Scripture in Song/Maranatha Music/Music Services/Song Solutions CopyCare, 14 Horsted Square, Uckfield, East Sussex TN22 1QG; info@songsolutions.org. Used by permission.

Christ is Alive, Let Christians Sing by Brian Wren. Stainer & Bell Ltd, London, England; www.stainer.co.uk.

Father, I Place into Your Hands by Jenny Hewer, copyright © 1975 Thankyou Music.*
*Adm. by worshiptogether.com songs, excl. UK and Europe, adm. by kingswaysongs.com; tym@kingsway.co.uk. Used by permission.

Forgive Our Sins, as We Forgive by Rosamond Herklots (1905–87). Verses 1 and 2 produced by permission of Oxford University Press. All rights reserved.

Great is Thy Faithfulness, words by Thomas O. Chisholm, copyright © 1923, ren. 1951, Hope Publishing Co., Carol Stream, IL 60188. All rights reserved. Used by permission.

He Lives by Alfred H. Ackley, © The Rodeheaver Co/Word Music LLC/ Song Solutions CopyCare, 14 Horsted Square, Uckfield, East Sussex TN22 1QG; info@songsolutions.org. Used by permission.

How Can We Sing With Joy to God by Brian Foley, copyright © 1971 by Faber Music Ltd, London. Reprinted from *New Catholic Hymnal* by permission of the publishers.

I, the Lord of Sea and Sky (Here I Am, Lord) by Daniel Schutte. Text and music © 1981, OCP. Published by OCP, 5536 NE Hassalo, Portland, OR 97213. All rights reserved. Used with permission.

I'd Rather Have Jesus by Rhea F. Miller and George Beverley Shea, © The Rodeheaver Co/Word Music LLC/Song Solutions CopyCare, 14 Horsted Square, Uckfield, East Sussex TN22 1QG; info@songsolutions.org. Used by permission.

Acknowledgements

In Christ Alone, words and music by Keith Getty and Stuart Townend, copyright © 2001 Kingsway Thankyou Music.*
*Adm. by worshiptogether.com songs, excl. UK & Europe, adm. by kingswaysongs.com; tym@kingsway.co.uk. Used by permission.

In God Alone, © Ateliers et Presses de Taizé, 71250 Taizé, France.

Jesus Calls Us Here to Meet Him, from John L. Bell and Graham Maule, *Love From Below* (Wild Goose Publications, 1989). Words and arrangement: John L. Bell and Graham Maule. Copyright © 1989 WGRG, Iona Community, Glasgow G2 3DH, Scotland, wgrg@iona.org.uk; www.wgrg.co.uk.

Let There Be Love Shared Among Us by Dave Bilbrough, copyright © 1979 Thankyou Music.*
*Adm. by worshiptogether.com songs, excl. UK and Europe, adm. by kingswaysongs.com; tym@kingsway.co.uk. Used by permission.

Let There Be Peace on Earth by Sy Miller and Jill Jackson, copyright © 1955, renewed 1983, by Jan-Lee Music (ASCAP). Administered in the UK by Chelsea Music Publishing Ltd.

Lord, for the Years Your Love by Timothy Dudley-Smith (b. 1926), © Timothy Dudley-Smith in Europe and Africa. Verses 1 and 3 reproduced by permission of Oxford University Press. All rights reserved.

Lord of All Hopefulness, words by Jan Struther (1901–53), from *Enlarged Songs of Praise*, 1931. Verse 2 reproduced by permission of Oxford University Press. All rights reserved.

Make Me a Blessing by Ira Wilson (words), © The Rodeheaver Co/Word Music LLC/Song Solutions CopyCare, 14 Horsted Square, Uckfield, East Sussex TN22 1QG; info@songsolutions.org. Used by permission.

Make Me a Channel of Your Peace, prayer of St Francis, dedicated to Mrs Frances Tracy. © 1967, OCP, 5536 NE Hassalo, Portland, OR 97213. All rights reserved. Used with permission.

Acknowledgements

O Lord My God, When I in Awesome Wonder (How Great Thou Art) by Stuart K. Hine, copyright © 1953 The Stuart Hine Trust/kingswaysongs.com.*
*Published by kingswaysongs.com worldwide (excl. North and South America); tym@kingsway.co.uk. Used by permission.

One More Step Along the World I Go by Sydney Carter. Stainer & Bell Ltd, London, England; www.stainer.co.uk.

Sing of the Lord's Goodness, © 1981, Ernest Sands. Published by OCP, 5536 NE Hassalo, Portland, OR 97213. All rights reserved. Used with permission.

Spirit of God, Unseen as the Wind, copyright © Scripture Union.

Such Love by Graham Kendrick, copyright © 1988 Make Way Music; www.grahamkendrick.co.uk.

Take This Moment, Sign and Space, from John L. Bell and Graham Maule, *Love From Below* (Wild Goose Publications, 1989). Words and music: John L. Bell and Graham Maule. Copyright © 1989 WGRG, Iona Community, Glasgow G2 3DH, Scotland, wgrg@iona.org.uk; www.wgrg.co.uk.

Tell Out My Soul by Timothy Dudley-Smith (b. 1926), © Timothy Dudley-Smith in Europe and Africa. Verse 1 reproduced by permission of Oxford University Press. All rights reserved.

The Wonder of It All by George Beverly Shea, © Word Music LLC/Song Solutions CopyCare, 14 Horsted Square, Uckfield, East Sussex TN22 1QG; info@songsolutions.org. Used by permission.

There is No Moment of My Life by Brian Foley, copyright © 1971 by Faber Music Ltd, London. Reprinted from *New Catholic Hymnal* by permission of the publishers.

We Are One in the Spirit (They'll Know We Are Christians by Our Love) by Peter Scholtes, © Fel Publications/Lorenz Publishing Co/Small Stone Media/Song Solutions Daybreak, 14 Horsted Square, Uckfield, East Sussex TN22 1QG; info@songsolutions.org. Used by permission.

You Shall Cross the Barren Desert (Be Not Afraid), © 1975, 1978, Robert J. Dufford SJ and OCP, 5536 NE Hassalo, Portland, OR 97213. All rights reserved. Used with permission.

Index of hymns

Index of hymns